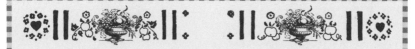

The Farmer's Wife

Harvest Cookbook

OVER 300 BLUE-RIBBON RECIPES!

D1607199

LELA NARGI, EDITOR

Voyageur Press

First published in 2010 by Voyageur Press, an imprint of MBI Publishing Company, 400 First Avenue North, Suite 300, Minneapolis, MN 55401 USA

Voyageur Press titles are also available at discounts in bulk quantity for industrial or sales-promotional use. For details write to Special Sales Manager at MBI Publishing Company, 400 First Avenue North, Suite 300, Minneapolis, MN 55401 USA.

To find out more about our books, visit us online at www.voyageurpress.com.

ISBN-13: 978-0-7603-3799-8

Editor: Melinda Keefe
Design Manager: Brenda C. Canales
Layout by: Helena Shimizu

Library of Congress Cataloging-in-Publication Data
The Farmer's wife harvest cookbook : over 300 blue-ribbon recipes! / edited by Lela Nargi.
    p. cm.
ISBN 978-0-7603-3799-8 (comb-plc)
1. Cookery. I. Nargi, Lela. II. Farmers wife.
TX714.F372 2010
641.5--dc22

                                        2010001189

Printed in China

Contents

Introduction 9

Read This First 13

Starting Out with a Hearty Breakfast 17

What to Cook for the Threshing Crew 39
The Main Staple: Bread 42
The Big Meal 48
Side Dishes 74
Dessert 92

Everyday Meals from Harvest-Time Bounty 117
July 118
August 130
September 142
October 152
November 156

Lazy Day Late Summer Picnics 161
Picnic Nibbles 164
Sandwiches 169
Salads 180
Cooking Out of Doors 200
Drinks 208

Index 223

HARVEST TIME
Short cuts

July 1936

Tradition has a way of asserting itself at harvest time. In the harvest meal contest conducted last year by the *Farmer's Wife* Magazine, we found that the meals planned by farm homemakers in 35 states fell into pretty general patterns.

In this contest we also asked, "Do you serve between-meal lunches in the field. Why or why not?" Other information which we asked for was for short cuts in preparing and serving harvest time meals. Such helpful suggestions were given that they are worthy of study even though you may not have harvesters to feed, for experiences learned under pressure of a heavy load of work are pretty valuable ones.

To the question, "Do you serve between-meal lunches in the field?" answers were 54 percent no, 40 percent yes, and 6 percent depends. If there were "young lads" in the crew, the farmer's wives felt they really needed extra food for strength. The pause seemed welcome— "It gives the men extra pep and energy for their hard work"; or "The men need a few minutes' rest and did not need to eat so much supper, so could rest better." Many said, "It is (or is not) the custom in our neighborhood," which settled the question. A number served a refreshing cold drink or fruit, "which is much better for the men than more cooked food."

Some lunches were very simple, as doughnuts and fruit punch, home-canned grape juice and cup cakes, cold buttermilk and ginger cookies. Other lunches included as much as two kinds of sandwiches, cakes, cookies, and coffee.

Some of the comments made by those who do not serve lunches were as follows: "this is a dairy section and our day in the field is not so long as in some places," or, "I do not serve lunches in the field for I have found that the men prefer good, hearty meals at regular hours to lunching." Another said, "I do not serve lunches. It is not customary in our locality and the men say it wastes their time, as well as mine."

When the harvesters were a long distance from the house, the noon meal was sometimes taken to the field. A Utah contributor wrote that their ranch was six miles from their home, so a hearty breakfast and

evening dinner were served at their house, with a lighter noon meal sent with the men when they left in the morning.

Mrs. H. W. Tanner of Wisconsin says they do not serve lunches in a mixed farming district where farmers exchange work, and quit early on account of chores. When they lived in the grain belt, however, she says, "we served lunch both morning and afternoon. Morning lunch always seemed superfluous and especially difficult. The 4 o'clock lunch, on the contrary, was a welcome respite. By then work was beginning to lag. The brief rest and lunch with its hot, stimulating coffee seemed to hearten the men for the remaining hours of daylight."

It was most satisfactory for the women to take lunch out with the car. It gave them a bit of change and fresh air, and more important, the food was protected, as far as possible, from drying out and the inevitable dust and flies. Foods were "hand" foods. Sandwiches were substantial and not messy—lettuce leaves omitted. Layer cakes were taboo. Cake was baked in paper baking cups or took the form of cookies or fried cakes. Coffee was in a close-covered shot-gun can, served with a long-handled dipper.

Short Cuts and Time Savers
Summarized and quoted from these farm women's letters are many helpful ideas which dealt with planning, equipment, and methods of serving.

Careful Planning
Plan ahead—write out menus and follow them.

Bake and cook a day ahead such foods as cookies, bread, rolls (reheated in paper sacks), baked beans, cakes which keep moist, and

salad dressing. Chickens may be cooked unless they are to be fried, and then just dressed, and ham boiled ahead. One reader says to make but not bake apple pies the day ahead, cover with waxed paper and put in the ice box overnight. This makes them extra crisp.

Early in the day, before it's hot, gather and prepare vegetables, bake pies and fresh cakes.

Two-in-one cooking: prepare potatoes for two or three meals at one time. Cook enough beets to serve pickled the second day. Prepare enough roast beef to serve cold or as a stew for a second meal.

Use canned meats, vegetables, and fruits as a time and labor saver for a large crew, especially when help is scarce or when the fresh supply is limited. Gallon fruit may be used for pies. Writes one, "I always can at least 25 quarts of baked beans for summer use."

Mix dry ingredients and lard ahead of time for pies and biscuits. Store in a cool place till needed, when liquid is added.

An emergency shelf, well stocked, takes care of the unexpected.

Use cream as a shortening for cakes and cookies.

After dinner is the time to prepare and bake casserole dishes to be used for supper, using the dinner stove. Supper then requires little heat.

Cook plenty and to spare, but not so many kinds of food.

Convenient Equipment

Use casseroles. Again and again came the comment that baking-serving dishes are a big help. They keep food hot, avoid last-minute dishing up, save dishes, and are the most attractive way to serve hot vegetables.

Use a basket for carrying supplies from cellar or storage place. Use trays to carry food from ice box to kitchen and from kitchen to table.

Pressure cookers save time, fuel, worry.

A pastry blender is invaluable for pies, biscuits, cake.

On dishwashing: "Buy a dish drainer and use it." "Also, I keep baking dishes washed up. It's not just the notion but a nerve tonic."

Have plenty of clean dishtowels and hot water ready.

Use a double boiler to keep gravy hot.

Use paper cases for cupcakes and make drop and ice-box cookies rather than rolled cookies.

Quick, Simple Serving

Provide plenty of clean towels and wash basins for the men's "wash up" before meals.

Have meals ready on time.

"We always have flowers on the table and find harvest men enjoy them as much as city businessmen would."

A serving table in the dining room for cold foods is a big help.

Set the table early, draw blinds, and keep dining room cool.

"We let each man take his plate with meat and potatoes as he passes through the kitchen. The rest of the food is put on to be passed."

Avoid confusion in passing by starting everything to the right.

Reset the table for the next meal as soon as dishes are washed, and cover with a clean cloth. Or stack clean dishes near the table and cover.

"If the hostess will be seated with the men, serving is much easier as she can have a tea cart with beverage, dessert, etc. at her side. An occasional word to men to pass things eliminates the necessity of being on her feet constantly when she has no help."

Drawn by
J. N.
Darling

Introduction

The *Farmer's Wife* was a monthly magazine published in Minnesota between the years 1893 and 1939. In an era long before the Internet and high-speed travel connected us all, the magazine aimed to offer community among hard-working rural women: to provide a forum for their questions and concerns, and to assist them in the day-to-day goings on about the farm—everything from raising chickens and slaughtering hogs, to managing scant funds and dressing the children, to keeping house and running the kitchen.

Unlike her urban counterparts, the farmer's wife wasn't just responsible for preparing meals for her immediate family—a daunting enough task in itself, especially when added to her myriad other chores. A farm in those days was dependent upon community, and at no time was this truer than at harvest time. In the busy summer months after the crops—sometimes hundreds of acres of them—had been hauled in by the family and perhaps a few neighbors, a farmer might hire a threshing crew of up to twelve men to assist in removing the edible parts of the grain from the chaff. This process could take as long as a week, during which time the crew would expect three hot, nourishing meals a day, and possibly also smaller, cold meals to bring with them out to the fields. These meals, of course, were provided by the farmer's wife.

She tackled the event—for it truly was an *event*, as you will discover when you read some of the firsthand accounts included in this book—of feeding the threshing crew with great seriousness, strict planning, and, if she was experienced, a tremendous amount of opinion about what should be served and how much of it.

In short, when it came to feeding the threshing crew, the farmer's wife wasn't messing around.

Which is not to say that summer was entirely joyless down on the farm. The children were on vacation from school after all, and after and in between the busiest work, the farmer's wife and her family enjoyed local Fourth of July parties, harvest celebrations, and picnics. Probably not so unlike you and your family, no matter where you live.

Included in this book are over three hundred recipes for feeding folks—and in some cases, a lot of folks—during the summer months. Some of the recipes will help you put together a simple, informal hot meal for friends and family; others will help you figure out what to do with your own garden and farmers' market bounty when it seems that the profusion of blackberries and tomatoes will never end; and still others will help you solve the riddle of what to bring along to, or even cook over an open flame at, that happiest of summer mealtime events—the picnic.

The recipes have been reprinted here much as they appeared on the pages of the magazine. Most recipes have been taken from issues spanning 1911–1939, and many were written by the magazine's own readers. In their language, they reflect the curious style and manners of their times, and herein lies a great deal of their charm, and the reason I have chosen to alter them as little as possible. Anyone accustomed to reading cookbooks will nevertheless feel right at home among the pages of this book. After all, the farmer's wife was nothing if not common-sensical, and so were her recipes.

Anyone new to cookbooks—and, more particularly, historical cookbooks—is advised to follow the golden rule of the recipe: read it thoroughly, start to finish, and preferably more than once, before embarking. Make sure you understand the instructions and the order in which they must be carried out; make sure you have all the ingredients at hand and assembled; and make sure to preheat your oven a good twenty to thirty minutes before you are ready to bake.

Wherever possible, I have attempted to abolish confusing, misleading, or laborious instructions. I've also substituted modern equivalents for obsolete measurements, such as the gill (4 ounces) and the teacup (8 ounces). More than anything, this book wants to be used, not merely perused and admired. So please use it! And know that as you do, you are baking up a bit of farmland history.

—Lela Nargi

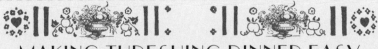

MAKING THRESHING DINNER EASY

July–August 1921
Mrs. L. Farrar

I am a farmer's wife. Every year I have to get dinner for the threshers. I used to think it a big job; now it's easy. Here's my plan:

My first point is to see that breads, cakes, and salad dressing are on hand the day before I must have threshers.

Second, I have my meal planned and supplies in the kitchen the evening before.

Third, I plan to secure an early start on the day of threshing so as to provide a time for rest from 10:00 to 10:30 a.m.

The menu I have found from experience to be the most successful is the following:

Roast beef with gravy	Soft-top pie
Baked beans	Cake with fresh fruit sauce
Mashed potatoes	or gelatin fruit salad
Bread and butter	Salad
Cabbage, peanut,	Iced tea or coffee
and banana salad	

I have noticed that the harvesters will seldom pass any of these dishes by.

In preparing the dinner I start early. While getting breakfast I put the beans on to parboil. Immediately after breakfast I bake the pies, having them out of the oven at 8 a.m. at which time the meat must go on to roast. A tough roast will spoil an otherwise good dinner. At the same time the beans should be put in to bake, for the secret of good beans is hours of baking. From this time till 10:00 I arrange the rest of the regular day's work. About 10:30 my friend and neighbor arrives, who relieves me of the care of the dining room, and leaves me free for overseeing the cooking. Then comes the real rush but, by preparing the meal in the proper order, hurry is avoided at the last minute.

By 11:45 the meat is ready to be cut, the gravy made, potatoes mashed, and salad mixed. The table is laid with the bread, cake, and pies. The bread and cake are wrapped with napkin if necessary, to protect them from drying winds. The iced tea. Butter and fruit gelatine are prepared for the table and on ice ready for immediate transfer, so when the harvesters file in to dinner after the noon whistle blows, the meal can be served in order without rush. Try this plan next time and I'm sure you will agree with me it's an easy task.

THE
FARMER'S WIFE
The Magazine for Farm Women

JULY, 1930

Read This First: How to Use This Book

All the recipes in this book are simple to execute. Inexperienced cooks are advised to read a recipe completely once or twice before embarking, and to assemble and prepare all ingredients in advance of cooking. Actually, this is sound advice for all cooks, regardless of experience.

Farm women once had an ample supply of bacon and other drippings readily at hand, kept in a coffee can and used almost daily. Most contemporary cooks don't keep their drippings, so oil or butter can be substituted as appropriate. When a recipe calls for both bacon and drippings, the fat left over from frying the bacon can of course be used for just this purpose.

The ever-thrifty farmer's wife made her own breadcrumbs from stale, leftover bread. Make your own by cutting stale bread into small cubes and storing the cubes in the freezer in a zip-top bag. When the bag is full, run the frozen bread cubes through a blender or food processor to pulverize. Freeze again until ready to use. To make buttered breadcrumbs (frequently called for in this book) mix with ⅛ c. melted butter per 1 c. crumbs.

Gravy would have been a common leftover in the kitchen of the farmer's wife—left over, that is, from the roasts and chops she so frequently prepared. Please don't use commercial canned gravy as a substitute for this relatively wholesome, homey product. See the recipe on page 70 for instructions on making your own gravy.

"I'LL HAVE NO ASHES IN MY KITCHEN EVEN IN WINTER!

Aside from cottage cheese, which could be readily produced by pouring hot water over thick, sour milk (a common farm product), the farmer's wife did not make much cheese, unless she was engaged in its commercial manufacture. She had ample access to "store" cheese, though, which is how she commonly referred to cheddar. Recipes in the *Farmer's Wife* magazine sometimes referred specifically to other types of cheese, such as American or Parmesan; mostly, though, the original recipes are vague in the type of cheese to use. Experienced or adventurous cooks are encouraged to follow their instincts as to what sort of cheese might be used in any dish.

"Seasonings" would have been understood by the farmer's wife to mean, first and foremost, salt and pepper. Efforts have been made in this book to differentiate between salt and pepper seasoning and the secondary meaning of the word, which includes other herbs, spices, and flavorings—these are listed separately on ingredients lists.

Honey was not necessarily a common farm staple—the farmer's wife more frequently used sugar in her cooking and baking. Some recipes calling for honey appeared in the magazine from time to time and were considered quite novel. Reference in these instances is almost always made to "strained" honey, which is the clear, liquid version most of us buy these days. The term "strained honey" applied to honey that had been removed from the comb and strained free of wax and crystals. Any store-bought honey not in the comb will suffice for the recipes here.

Most farmers' wives canned their own home-grown fruit. Substitute fresh fruit or high-quality store-bought canned or jarred fruit.

Onion juice, once very much in favor, was a product of the farm kitchen. To make it, see the instructions on page 57. Otherwise, substitute onion powder or onion salt to taste.

In any recipe, shortening can be substituted for lard; "fat" can be interpreted as "butter"—use accordingly.

Quite a number of the original *Farmer's Wife* baking recipes call for sour milk. According to Sandra Oliver, editor of *Food History News*, sour milk was a naturally occurring product on farms in the days of pre-pasteurization. And it was very useful for baking. "The acidity in the sour milk interacted with the alkaline in the baking soda to make the gas that raised baked goods," she explains. I've substituted buttermilk in the recipes that call for sour milk. If you'd like to make your own sour milk, add 1 tbsp. vinegar to 1 c. "sweet" milk (a term the *Farmer's Wife* used to differentiate it from "sour" milk).

Always sift flour once before measuring.

1 pint = 2 c.
1 quart = 4 c.
1 peck = 8 qts.

Finally, the farmer's wife was a keen proponent of white sauce, which she used either as the foundation or a thickener for almost every kind of dish imaginable—from stews and soups to tomato sauce and nut butters. You can find instructions for making White Sauce on page 89. Every attempt has been made to set down the recipes here in the format in which they originally appeared in the magazine, but many contemporary cooks will doubtless feel compelled to completely omit white sauce in its guise as thickener or enricher from many of these recipes, and few recipes will suffer for it.

Starting Out with a Hearty Breakfast

Systematic planning may do much to save time in breakfast getting. The cereal may be entirely or partly cooked the evening before, the dry ingredients for hot bread mixed, pans greased, the fire "laid" and the table set.

The brown bread made in quantity will keep several days and the loaf may be steamed again in a short time. Or it may be sliced, spread out on a baking tin and heated quickly in the oven. Sometimes it is served with sausage, heated in the greased pan in which the sausage was cooked. This is substantial enough for the men working hard out of doors.

—The Farmer's Wife Magazine

These recipes may be doubled, even quadrupled, to feed large "crews" of friends and family.

❦ Breakfast Cocoa
October 1917

For each cupful use:
1 tsp. cocoa powder
1 tsp. sugar
few grains salt
1 c. milk

Mix the cocoa, sugar, and salt. Slowly add the boiling milk. Stir until the mixture is well-blended. The boiling brings out all the flavor and renders the starch in the cocoa more nutritious and digestible. The use of all milk makes a richer beverage of high food value.

❦ Oatmeal with Bran
November 1938

1 c. water
1½ c. milk
1 c. oatmeal
½ tsp. salt
½ c. bran

Scald water and milk, then add oatmeal and salt, stirring. Cook 3–5 minutes. Just before serving add bran. Serve with Different Bacon (see below).

❦ Different Bacon
November 1938

Slice bacon not too thin, dip into milk then flour. Fry on hot, greased skillet over medium flame till brown. This makes a heartier meat than usual.

❦ Apple Fritters

September 1929

1 ⅓ c. flour
2 tsp. baking powder
¼ tsp. salt
⅔ c. milk
1 well-beaten egg
2 medium-sized sour apples

Mix and sift dry ingredients, then add milk and egg gradually. Core and cut apples into eighths, then slice eighths into small pieces and stir into batter. Drop by spoonfuls and fry in deep fat. Drain well.

❦ Corn Fritters

November 1912

1 c. corn, cut off the cob
2 c. flour
pinch salt
1 tbsp. sugar
1 ½ tbsp. baking powder
enough water to make thick batter dough

Mix all together and drop by spoonfuls into a pan half full of hot oil. Cook until nicely browned on all sides. Drain on paper towels. Serve with maple syrup.

❧ Sour Cream Crullers
August 1916

½ c. butter
1½ c. sugar
1 small egg
1 tsp. baking soda
½ c. sour cream
2½ c. flour
a little grated nutmeg
powdered sugar

Cream the butter and sugar, add the egg, then the soda dissolved in sour cream and the flour. Mix well, adding more flour if necessary so as to make a dough that will roll out easily (it should be as soft as can be handled). Roll out to ¼ inch thickness, shape with a cutter, and fry in deep hot fat to a golden brown. Drain on thick brown paper for a moment and roll in powdered sugar while still warm. Sprinkle nutmeg on top. These crullers, when properly made, are not as liable to absorb the grease as a recipe in which more shortening is used.

❧ Sallie's Rye Dough Dabs
November 1928

2 c. rye flour
1 c. white flour
3 heaping tsp. sugar
1 egg
1¼ c. milk
1 tsp. cream of tartar
½ tsp. baking soda
salt

Mix all ingredients, shape into small balls, and fry like doughnuts in hot fat till golden brown. Drain on paper towels or brown paper.

❧ Sour Milk Biscuits
November 1912

1 qt. flour
1 tsp. salt
1 tsp. baking soda

Sift together then rub into this, using the tips of the fingers only, 1 large tbsp. butter. Gradually stir into this thick sour cream to make a soft dough (½ to ¾ c.). When just stiff enough to be handled, mix it well by cutting through with a broad knife until it looks spongy. Turn it out onto a floured board, pat it with a rolling pin to ½ inch thick, cut it with a big biscuit cutter, and bake immediately at 375°F until golden—about 12–20 minutes. The dough should be handled with the hands as little as possible. When properly made these will "melt in the mouth."

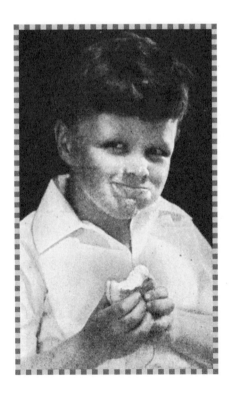

GOOD COOK'S CORNER
Our Foods Editor Tells of Tricks with Muffins
that Save Time and Texture
May 1934

I'm willing to make a wager that in almost any group of farm women, the regular biscuit makers will outnumber the regular muffin makers two to one. Why? Do muffins seem like too much work? Do they turn out wrong, with queer peaks and long tunnels?

There are many meals, of course, when biscuits are just the thing, but many times, too, muffins would be a happy choice.

Muffins should be stirred up in a hurry—it is *one, two, three*, and then pop them in the oven.

1. Mix together all the dry ingredients.
2. Mix together all the wet ingredients.
3. Combine the two mixtures.

Of course, if you want a dress-up muffin, you can mix them as you do a cake—cream the fat and sugar, etc. But when you want a *quick* bread, do it as directed above and you'll have light, delicious muffins ready in a flash.

In fact, the biggest single fault of muffin makers is that they *overmix*. Stir *just until dry ingredients are dampened*, but do not smooth or free from lumps, and then *stop*. Studies at the University of Chicago showed that on the average 20 seconds of mixing gave the best results.

Try this experiment yourself some day when you feel venturesome: measure and mix according to the recipe, and when ingredients are just dampened nicely and still lumpy, take out batter to fill four to six tins. Then stir what is left a few seconds longer; take out two more; stir some more and fill another row. Bake them all together and see for yourself how many stirs you should give to secure an even texture. Round tops usually go with even texture and peaked tops with tunnels.

You will notice that in the recipe below [see Foundation Recipe for Muffins, pg. 24], the fat is added to the egg and milk mixture. You may use cooking oil or melted fat as butter, but see that the milk is not so cold that the fat hardens when it is poured in.

To speed up oiling of muffin tins, put them in a warm place while the supplies are being assembled. Use a brush (a nickel or dime well invested) or a bit of waxed paper. If the pans are the heavy iron kind, have them heated through before dropping in the batter.

Good Cooks' Corner

Foundation Recipe for Muffins
May 1934

I	II
2 c. sifted flour	1 egg
2 tsp. baking powder	1 c. milk
2 tbsp. sugar	3 tbsp. melted butter
½ tsp. salt	
Sift together into a large bowl	Beat egg till foamy, add milk and fat

III

Pour wet ingredients, all at once, into the dry and stir vigorously until dry ingredients are just dampened. The batter should *not* be entirely smooth. Fill buttered muffin tins two-thirds full with as little extra stirring as possible. Bake at 425°F for 20 minutes.

Variations:

With sour milk instead of sweet: decrease baking powder to 1 tsp. and sift ½ tsp. baking soda in with dry ingredients. If milk is quite thick, you might need more than 1 c.

With sour cream: Use 1 c. in place of milk, omit the butter, and follow the directions for sour milk.

For whole wheat, graham, or bran muffins: use 1 c. dark flour or bran and 1 c. sifted white flour. Increase baking powder to 3 tsp.; a little less milk is needed with coarse flour or bran. ¼ c. brown sugar may be substituted for white, or sugar may be left out and ¼ c. molasses added to the liquid ingredients.

Nut or fruit muffins: Add ½ c. chopped dates, raisins, or nuts to either plain or dark muffins. Mix thoroughly with the dry ingredients before liquids are added.

❧ Graham Muffins
March 1912

To 2 c. milk add beaten yolks of two eggs, stir with 3 c. graham flour with which 1 tsp. sugar, 1 tsp. salt, and 2 tsp. baking powder have been mixed. Fold in the beaten egg whites last and bake in buttered muffin pans at 350°F for up to ½ hour.

❧ Honey Bran Flake Muffins
April 1935

1¼ c. flour
1½ tsp. baking powder
½ tsp. baking soda
¼ tsp. salt
4 tbsp. honey

¾ c. buttermilk
1 egg, well beaten
3 tbsp. melted butter
1 c. bran flakes

Sift together flour, baking powder and soda, and salt. Combine honey, buttermilk, egg, and butter. Add to flour, adding only enough to dampen all the flour. Add bran flakes. Bake in greased muffin pans at 425°F for 20 minutes.

❧ Potato Muffins
May 1918

4 tbsp. butter
2 tbsp. sugar
1 egg, well beaten
1 c. mashed potato
2 c. flour
3 tsp. baking powder
1 c. milk

Cream the butter and sugar, add the well-beaten egg, then the potato, and mix thoroughly. Stir in sifted dry ingredients alternately with milk. Bake at 350°F in buttered muffin tins for 25 to 30 minutes.

❦ Banana Bread
March 1930

½ c. butter
1 c. sugar
2 eggs, well beaten
3 bananas, mashed fine
8 tbsp. milk
2 c. flour sifted with 1 tsp. baking soda

Cream butter and sugar, add eggs and banana, and mix thoroughly. Add milk, flour, and baking soda. Pour into a buttered loaf pan and bake at 350°F for 1 hour.

❦ Two Good German Coffee Cakes

April 1913

Contributed by Sarah E. Seel

Dissolve 1½ cakes of yeast in ½ pt. equal parts warm water and milk. Beat stiff with a little flour and set to rise. Let rise to twice its height. Sift 2 qts. flour into a bowl. Salt to taste. Stir in 1 tbsp. cinnamon. Melt 2 c. butter into ¾ pt. warm milk and stir into flour, mixing thoroughly with a wooden spoon. Beat in one egg. Now pour in yeast, beating with a spoon until dough loosens from edge of bowl. Leave in bowl and set in cool place overnight. Next morning, grease two 8-inch pans. Pour dough on floured board, kneading till firm. Cut off a medium-sized piece, roll until ½ inch thick. Butter thinly, then sprinkle with cinnamon, sugar, and raisins. Roll up and place in pan to rise. Bake at 350°F for 20–30 minutes, till done.

Take another piece, roll as above, spread with good jelly, and lay flat in the bottom of a pan. Roll out another piece the same size and lay on top of first layer. Set to rise. Bake when well-up.

These recipes make an extremely good cake, which will keep fresh for 10 days.

❦ German Kuchen (Coffee Cake)
April 1938

1 pkg. active dry yeast	1 tsp. salt
¾ c. sugar	1 egg, slightly beaten
¼ c. lukewarm water	½ tsp. nutmeg
1 c. milk	½ c. raisins
3 c. flour, sifted	¼ c. shortening, melted
1 c. milk	

Topping:

1½ tbsp. butter, softened	1 tbsp. brown sugar
2 tbsp. granulated sugar	½ tsp. cinnamon, if desired

Dissolve yeast and 2 tbsp. sugar in lukewarm water. Scald milk and cool until lukewarm. Add dissolved yeast and sugar. Sift flour before and after measuring. Add half the flour and beat thoroughly. Cover, and allow sponge to rise in a warm place until full of bubbles, about 45 minutes. Add remainder of sugar, salt, slightly beaten egg, nutmeg, raisins, and melted shortening. Add remainder of flour gradually, beating thoroughly after each addition. Let stand 10 minutes. Turn onto lightly floured board and knead until smooth and elastic. Place in bowl, cover, and let rise until double in size, about 1½ hours. Shape into loaves to fit greased pans. Let rise until light—about 45 minutes. For topping, spread with soft butter. Sprinkle with sugars and cinnamon. Bake in moderately hot oven (400°F) for 30 minutes. Remove from pans and allow to cool before storing.

❦ Cinnamon Rolls
1934

Use recipe for Baking Powder Biscuits (pg. 52). Lightly roll dough out to ¼ inch thick, spread with soft butter, then sprinkle with a mixture of sugar and cinnamon. Roll up from the long side like a jelly roll. Cut slices ½ inch thick and lay flat on buttered baking sheets. Bake at 450°F for about 12 minutes.

Orange Biscuits
1934

Use recipe for Baking Powder Biscuits (pg. 52), substituting orange juice for part of the milk. Roll out to ⅓ inch thick, cut, and transfer to baking sheet. On top of each biscuit put a cube of sugar that has been soaked in orange juice long enough to absorb some of it but not to dissolve. Grate orange rind over top. Bake at 450°F for about 12 minutes.

Sour Milk Griddle Cakes
1934

2 c. flour
2 tbsp. cornmeal
1 tsp. salt
1 tsp. baking soda
1 tbsp. sugar
2 to 2⅓ c. buttermilk
1 egg, beaten
2 tbsp. melted butter

Mix and sift dry ingredients together. Add buttermilk, egg, and melted butter. Mix well. Drop by spoonfuls onto a buttered, hot griddle, flipping to cook on the second side when the first side is nicely browned.

❦ Rice Cakes

October 1913

2 c. flour
2 c. cooked rice
4 eggs
2 tbsp. melted butter
1 tsp. salt
4 tsp. baking powder
3 c. milk

Mix all the ingredients together. Cook on hot, greased griddle, as for Sour
Milk Griddle Cakes (pg. 29).

❦ Rhode Island Johnny Cakes

November 1928

*The meal used for these is made from white cap corn, stone ground by water
power or wind because this method is slower and does not heat the meal.
This is a special Rhode Island meal which is now shipped in small quantities to
many localities. It must be used quickly as it soon deteriorates.*

—The Farmer's Wife Magazine

Put 2 c. cornmeal into a bowl with 1 tsp. salt. Have the teakettle at the
jumping boil and pour boiling water over the meal a little at a time, beating
vigorously until the meal is scalded but not thinned. Then, thin with milk
to the consistency of a drop batter. Drop on a well-greased, hot griddle
and cook like griddle cakes. For huckleberry Johnny Cakes, add ¾ c.
huckleberries to this recipe.

❧ Slappers
May 1912

Put 2 c. yellow cornmeal, 1 tsp. butter, the same of sugar, and ½ tsp. salt into a bowl and thoroughly wet it with boiling milk. Let cool, then add two beaten eggs and enough cold milk to make a very thin batter. Drop by spoonfuls onto a hot, greased griddle and brown on both sides. Serve hot with butter and maple syrup.

❧ Waffles par Excellence
October 1913

4 c. flour
2 c. milk
4 eggs
2 tbsp. melted butter
4 tbsp. baking powder
1 tsp. salt

Mix well and cook on hot irons.

❧ French Toast
1934

2 eggs
½ tsp. salt
1 tsp. sugar

½ c. milk
6 slices stale bread

Beat eggs slightly, then add salt, sugar, and milk. Dip bread in mixture. Cook in small amount of butter in frying pan till golden brown on each side. Serve with bacon strips and maple syrup. An excellent breakfast dish.

❦ French Fruit Toast

March 1930
Contributed by Mrs. E.R.S., South Carolina

2 eggs
½ tsp. salt
1 tsp. sugar
1 c. milk
8–12 thin slices bread
jam or preserves

Beat eggs; add salt, sugar, and milk. Spread bread with jam and fit two slices together like a sandwich. Dip into egg mixture and cook on hot, buttered griddle over medium flame until lightly browned. Turn and brown the other side and serve hot.

❦ Peanut Butter Toast

September 1917

4 tbsp. melted butter
4 tbsp. flour
8 tbsp. peanut butter
milk to thin
salt and pepper to taste
4 slices toasted bread
4 slices cooked bacon

Heat butter in saucepan. Add flour, stir till smooth, then add peanut butter. Mix thoroly, add milk enough to thin slightly; season with salt and pepper to taste. Pour over thin slices of toast, place a slice of bacon on each slice of toast, and serve at once.

Toasted Cheese with Bacon
October 1926

Slice bread ½ inch thick and cover with thin slices of cheese. Sprinkle with salt and paprika and lay two slices of bacon on each piece. Place on a cookie sheet and bake at 400°F until bacon is crisp and cheese melted. If you have a use for hard breadcrumbs, the crusts may be removed from the bread, dried, and ground.

Corn Scramble
May 1926

¼ lb. bacon
1 pt. corn kernels
6 eggs
1 c. milk
salt and pepper to taste

Cut bacon in pieces and fry with corn. Leave 2 tbsp. fat in pan. Beat eggs slightly, add milk, and cook over low heat till creamy and thick, stirring all the time. Add seasoning to taste and serve on toast or boiled noodles.

🌿 Eggs à la King
May 1931

2 tbsp. butter
1 diced pimiento
½ c. chopped mushrooms
4 tbsp. flour
1 tsp. salt
2 c. milk
6 hard-cooked eggs, cut lengthwise
6 slices toasted bread

Melt the butter, add pimiento and mushrooms, and brown slightly. Add flour and salt and cook, stirring constantly. Add the milk gradually, stirring all the time, until thickened. Arrange the hard-cooked eggs on toast and then pour hot sauce over them. Serve at once.

🌿 Creamed Eggs and Bacon on Toast
April 1932

1 tbsp. butter
1 tbsp. flour
½ tsp. salt
½ tsp. pepper
1 c. milk
6 hard-cooked eggs, quartered
6 strips bacon, broiled till crisp
6 slices toasted bread

Make white sauce by melting butter in a skillet, stirring in flour till lightly browned, adding salt and pepper, then stirring in milk in a steady stream till thickened. Add eggs, then pour mixture over toast and top each piece with one or two strips of bacon.

❦ Baked Eggs and Greens
April 1932

2 c. cooked greens, like spinach or mustard
¼ c. grated Parmesan cheese
4 eggs
½ c. White Sauce (pg. 89)

Put layer of greens in bottom of baking dish. Sprinkle with grated cheese. Break eggs over top of greens and cover with White Sauce. Bake at 300°F till cheese is melted and eggs set.

❦ Bread Omelet
March 1917

3 tbsp. fine breadcrumbs
6 tbsp. milk
12 eggs
¾ tsp. salt
pepper

Let crumbs soak in milk till soft. Beat eggs till very light, add salt and pepper then breadcrumbs, beating constantly till mixture is poured into pan. The beating keeps it from being crumbly. Butter a frying pan and when hot, pour in the omelet. Turn pan slowly to cook the omelet evenly. When well puffed up, set for 1 minute in broiler to cook the top. Turn out on a hot platter and serve. For a sweet omelet leftover cake, crumbs may be used.

❧ Ham Omelet

April 1932

4 eggs
½ tsp. salt
¼ tsp. pepper
4 tsp. butter, melted
4 tbsp. milk
½ c. chopped ham

Separate yolks from whites. To well-beaten yolks add salt and pepper, butter, and milk. Fold in stiffly beaten egg whites and chopped ham, pour into hot, buttered skillet, and cook over low flame till bottom is golden brown and omelet puffed up. Then, set in oven at 350°F for 5–10 minutes to cook top. Crease through center and fold in half. Serve at once. Chopped ham, crisp diced bacon, dried beef, or sliced peaches, may be put between halves instead of adding when mixing.

🌾 Huevos Rancheros
February 1930

Heat 1 tbsp. lard, butter, or oil in a thick iron pan, then slip in six fresh eggs, taking care that each egg is whole and separate. Pour ½ c. Chile Sauce (see below) over these, put on a tight lid, and cook over moderate fire till tops of eggs are glazed over. If hard eggs are preferred, continue cooking till yolks are hard.

🌾 Chile Sauce

2 tbsp. dried chile pepper
2 tbsp. pure hog lard
2 tsp. flour
1 clove garlic
1 slice onion

Soak the dried peppers in hot water to cover till soft, having first opened them to remove most of the seeds. Then, with a spoon, scrape out the meaty part, discarding the tough outer skin. Mash this pulp fine before measuring. (Although many chile powders are on the market, the pulp of the dried peppers, prepared in this manner, is to be preferred in making any dish seasoned with chile.) Heat the lard slowly, stir in the flour, and add enough hot water to make a gravy. Then, stir in the pepper pulp and simmer till thoroughly blended. Add one clove of garlic and a slice of onion to this while it cooks, but be sure to remove them before serving. A mere flavor of each is sufficient.

What to Cook for the Threshing Crew

For an accustomed cook, the work of preparing meals for the extra harvest hands presents no special problem. It is a matter of assembling food and promptly preparing it in appetizing ways.

To nearly every farmwoman, however, comes an appalling first time when she finds herself faced by the question of how much she must prepare for a given number of men. To this question is now added our national duty of economy. We are asked to prepare for our tables not so much what we best enjoy as what will most acceptably and economically nourish bodies for the work they must do.

Feeding the harvest helpers is hard for the woman who cannot have suitable appliances and has to depend on makeshifts. Among the most helpful utensils is a three- or four-gallon double boiler for making soups, gravies, and puddings; also a large steam cooker, which will take care of fifteen or twenty loaves of brown bread or steamed pudding, at once.

Beware of trying to fill up hungry men with foods that take much time to prepare. One should not try to serve pies often, unless there is plenty of help. Rolling crust is slow work even for a swift pie maker.

Three gallons of tapioca cream can be made at once in a big double boiler, almost as easily as one quart. When milk is available, it is no more expensive than pie and is as nourishing.

In the same way a large quantity of berry pudding may be mixed at once. A shortcake is more quickly handled than a pie crust. When it is possible to buy bread from a bakery during harvest time, the women of the farm should not be expected to make it. Doughnuts require considerable handling but little more than biscuit or muffins, and usually are more satisfactory.

The more variety we can give in the grain foods, the less meat will be required. Try to serve biscuit, dumplings, or squares of pie crust and stuffings with meats and fish to make a less quantity satisfying.

—How Much and What Kinds of Foods Harvest Hands Need
by Anna Barrows, July 1917

HOW MUCH FOOD WILL YOU NEED?

I am reproducing here the table [from the Department of Household Sciences of the University of Illinois] which gives in ounces a balanced ration for a man of 150 pounds. A little study of the table as a whole will help the housewife to understand how this balance is preserved and how to estimate what she will need to furnish for five men or twenty-five.

Men at Severe Work

Kind of Food	Ounces
Breakfast:	
Apple sauce	4.00
Oatmeal	2.00
Cream	2.15
Sugar	0.56
Sausage (pork)	2.00
Bread	2.60
Butter	0.50
Potatoes	4.00
Coffee (1 cup)	0.40
Sugar	0.28
Cream	1.07
Total	19.56
Dinner:	
Boiled ham	3.00
Potatoes	4.00
Sweet potatoes	4.00
Turnips	4.30

Corn bread	5.20
Bread	1.30
Butter	0.75
Cold slaw	1.33
Pie, mince	4.00
Coffee (1 cup)	0.40
Sugar	0.28
Cream	1.07
Total	29.63

Supper:

Dried beef (creamed)	1.00
Cream	1.07
Fried potatoes	2.40
Bread	1.30
Butter	0.75
Apple sauce	4.00
Ginger bread	4.00
Milk, skimmed	9.40
Total	23.92
Total for day	73.11

The Main Staple: Bread

Bread and bread products were critical staples at every meal during harvest time. Some farmers' wives were of the opinion that bread should be bought in large quantities from a local bakery (no doubt these were the women living in close proximity to town). Most seem to have baked it—a lot of it—every morning themselves.

❦ Quick Graham Bread
February 1932

2 c. graham flour
½ c. white flour
5 tsp. baking powder
1 tsp. salt
4 tbsp. melted fat
1½ c. milk
½ c. molasses or ⅓ c. sugar
½ c. nutmeats

Mix and sift flours, baking powder, and salt. Then add fat, milk, molasses, and nutmeats. Turn into buttered bread pan and bake 45–50 minutes in moderately hot oven (400°F).

❦ Steamed Brown Bread

July–August 1921

1½ c. graham flour
2 c. cornmeal
3 tsp. baking powder
1½ tsp. salt

⅓ c. currants
⅔ c. raisins
2 c. milk
⅔ c. molasses

Mix together flour, meal, baking powder and salt, currants, and raisins. Add milk and molasses and beat well. Pour into greased loaf pans. Fill slightly over half full of batter. Steam 3 hours.

❦ Whole Wheat or Cracked Wheat Bread

1934

1 qt. milk
⅓ c. brown sugar or honey
6 tbsp. butter
2 tbsp. salt
2 cakes compressed yeast
(substitute 2 pkgs. active
dry yeast)

¼ c. lukewarm water
6 c. whole-wheat flour
3 c. white flour
    OR
4 c. white flour and 4–5 c. coarser
    wheat flour

Scald milk in a double boiler with sugar, butter, and salt. Cool to lukewarm. Soak yeast in water and add milk in a bowl. Add enough whole-wheat flour to make a batter. Beat thoroughly; add rest of whole-wheat and white flour to knead. The dough should be of a softer consistency than for white bread but not actually sticky. Knead for 10 to 15 minutes; put into a greased bowl; cover; let rise at a temperature of 80–85°F until double in bulk. Knead down slightly without adding more flour; cover; let rise again until double. Make into loaves and put in well-greased individual bread pans. Brush top with melted fat. Cover and let rise until double in bulk. Bake until a golden brown in a moderately hot oven (400°F). Yield: three loaves of 1¾ lbs. each before baking.

Table for Quick Breads

	Milk	Flour	Fat	Eggs	Baking Powder	Sugar	Salt	Baking Time
Popovers (8)	1 c.	1 c.	½ tbsp.	2			⅓ tsp.	40-60 Min.
Waffles (4 to 8)	1 c.	1⅓ c.	4 tbsp.	2	2 tsp.		½ tsp.	4-5 min.
Griddle cakes (12)	1 c.	1½ c.	2 tbsp.	1	3 tsp.	1 tbsp.	½ tsp.	3-4 min.
Muffins (12)	1 c.	2 c.	2-4 tbsp.	1	3 tsp.	2-3 tbsp.	½ tsp.	25-30 min.
Biscuits (12)	1 c.	3 c.	6 tbsp.		5-6 tsp.		1 tsp.	10-12 min.

Sweet Rolls
April 1938

1 c. milk, scalded
1 c. lukewarm water
2 pkgs. active dry yeast
½ c. butter
⅔ c. sugar
1 tsp. salt
2 eggs, beaten
grated rind and juice of ½ lemon
⅛ tsp. nutmeg
about 7 c. sifted flour

Scald milk and cool to lukewarm. Pour lukewarm water over yeast, stir, and let stand 10 minutes. Cream together butter, sugar, and salt, add beaten eggs, lemon juice and rind, and nutmeg. Combine liquids, add 3 c. flour, and beat smooth. Add the butter-sugar mixture and more flour to make a soft dough. Knead smooth but keep as soft as can be handled without sticking. Let dough rise in a cozy, warm place until doubled. Shape into rolls at once. Bake at 400°F for about 20 minutes.

❦ Butterhorn Rolls
April 1937

1 c. milk, scalded
2 tbsp. sugar
1 c. lukewarm water
1 cake compressed yeast (substitute 1 pkg. active dry yeast)
7 to 8 c. sifted flour
½ c. fat
½ c. sugar
6 egg yolks
1 tbsp. salt

Scald milk with 2 tbsp. sugar and cool to lukewarm. Add water and yeast that has been mixed with part of the water. Add 3 c. flour to make a spongy batter. Beat, let stand until light. Cream fat and sugar, add egg yolks, and beat until light and fluffy. Add to sponge with rest of flour and salt. Knead lightly, cover, and let stand in warm place until double in bulk. Divide in three pieces, then roll out each one in ⅓-inch-thick rounds. Spread with soft butter, then cut in sixteen pie-shaped pieces. Beginning at large end, roll up each section with point at top, place on greased tin, brush top with egg beaten with water, and let stand, covered, until double in bulk. Bake 20 minutes at 425°F.

PILLSBURY FLOUR MILLS COMPANY
MINNEAPOLIS, U. S. A.

One of the family

❦ Popovers
November 1936

4 eggs, beaten slightly
1 c. milk
1 c. water
2⅓ c. sifted bread flour
1 tsp. salt
2 tsp. sugar

To eggs add two-thirds of liquid, then all of flour, salt, and sugar. (That's right, there's no baking powder.) Beat until smooth, then add rest of liquid. When blended, pour in warm, thoroughly greased pans. Fill muffin pans half full, deep custard cups or popover pan scarcely more than one-third full. Bake smaller tins, such as muffin pans, 25–30 minutes, deeper tins 35 minutes at 450–475°F, a really hot oven. Serve piping hot with butter. The popovers will pop up in 15 or 20 minutes, and the additional baking makes the thin walls crisp and brown. Serve as breakfast or hot supper bread. On occasion, fill with creamed chicken or chipped beef in cream.

SAMPLE MEALS FOR THRESHING DAYS
July 1917

Monday
Breakfast: Cracked wheat and cream, omelet, bread, coffee, doughnuts. Dinner: Chicken fricassee with dumplings, rice with tomato, green peas, cucumbers, peach ice cream, cake. Supper: Toasted herring with potato salad, cheese toast, quick biscuits and berries.

Tuesday
Breakfast: Brown bread and baked beans, ginger cookies, coffee. Dinner: Stuffed beef, baked potatoes, creamed onions, pickles, steamed berry pudding with sauce. Supper: Chicken with rice, salt codfish hash, stewed rhubarb, cake.

Wednesday
Breakfast: Sausage, cornbread, stewed prunes, berries, coffee. Dinner: Soup, roast pork, browned potatoes, beets, peach tapioca. Supper: Baked hash, salmon salad, molasses gingerbread.

Thursday
Breakfast: Creamed dried beef, potatoes, bread, berries, coffee. Dinner: Ham and eggs, mashed potatoes, string beans, creamy rice. Supper: Clam chowder, hot pilot bread, peach shortcake.

Friday
Breakfast: Minced ham and eggs on toast, doughnuts, coffee. Dinner: Bean soup, fish, potatoes, peas, squash, lemon pie (with two crusts). Supper: Lamb stew, cucumbers, graham bread, boiled samp with sirup.

Saturday
Breakfast: Creamed salt codfish, hashed potatoes, muffins, coffee. Dinner: Hamburg steaks, macaroni and cheese, tomatoes with lettuce or meat pie, Dutch apple cake with lemon sauce. Supper: baked beans with corned beef, brown bread, cucumber relish, cookies, berries.

Sunday
Breakfast: Cereal with bananas, griddle cakes with sirup, coffee. Dinner: roast lamb, mashed potatoes, shelled beans, tomatoes, jellied peaches, watermelon. Supper: Cold corned beef, vegetable salad, bread, berries.

The Big Meal

For the farmer's wife and her family and crew, the big meal, known as "dinner," would have been served around the noon hour. A smaller, lighter meal known as "supper" was served in the evening, once the work of the day was accomplished. Chicken, an inexpensive and plentiful farm staple, was the most common component of the big meal.

TABLE TALK
HUNGRY HARVESTERS MEALS
BIG DINNERS IN HOT WEATHER
August 1914
Jessie F. Stewart

In these days when help is almost out of the question on the farm, it often happens that the housewife, with but a few hours' previous notice, finds herself obliged to get up a dinner for hay hands, harvesters, or threshers. And she must do it alone.

In cold weather this big dinner would not prove so formidable, for she would know that she was going to have the men sometime during the week and could prepare many eatables in advance. In summer this could not be done.

If the housekeeper is content to use only those dishes which are easiest to prepare and simple as to serving, she may get up a very nourishing and appetizing dinner with but a few hours' notice.

One of our favorite dinners on the farm was fried chicken—not the kind you are thinking of perhaps, but a much simpler dish. We used two to four old hens, depending on the crowd we were cooking for. If time was limited, we skinned them; otherwise they were scalded and plucked, cut up as for boiling, and put on to boil about nine o'clock. At eleven they were done enough for the frying.

In the oven we put a big dripping pan, or two small ones, with a generous portion of lard or drippings. When this fat was piping hot, we

dipped each piece of the boiled hen in flour and placed it in the pan till all was in.

When the pan was put in the oven to fry till the chicken was brown on one side, it was then turned over and a big batch of baking powder biscuits laid over the top to bake. When the biscuits were brown on top, a gravy, made by stirring three tablespoons of flour into the boiling liquor, was poured over the pan and allowed to boil up for three minutes.

If you have timed your work correctly, you will pour the gravy over just as the men are coming to the house to wash. The chicken is heaped on large platters and the biscuits arranged about the edge. The gravy may need a bit of milk to thin. It is served in separate bowls.

With the chicken and gravy are served huge dishes of mashed potato, one of the easiest dishes to prepare, as it can be made ready after the chicken is on to cook.

As an extra vegetable, we usually had a large dish of sliced tomatoes, lots of them; sliced cucumbers with vinegar, or stewed tomatoes, all of which are easier to prepare in a hurry than string beans, corn, peas, and so forth.

Sometimes we served the chicken simply boiled with noodles or dumplings, and thus, having the oven free, baked beans as a second vegetable, since they need very little attention once they are in the oven.

Since you will have a pretty good idea that you are to have men to cook for soon, always see that your bread supply is ample. The biscuits, on meat, help out in the event of a shortage. Plenty of sweet milk and cream and nice, sweet butter should be on hand. Coffee may be ground up and kept for weeks in a closed jar. Plenty of clean towels, dish towels, and table linen may be kept always ready for the emergency dinner.

About all that is necessary is to keep calm, plan a simple dinner as you would for your own family, and multiply it by the number of extras and go at it just as for an ordinary family dinner.

❧ Southern Fried Chicken

March 1938

The most common fault in frying chicken is to allow too short a time for thorough cooking. The outside should be crisp brown, the inside moist and tender. First the age and tenderness of the chicken must be decided. For best results, use generous amount of fat in a fairly deep, heavy skillet and put in thicker pieces first. If pieces are turned frequently and fried slowly at the last, young chicken will cook through this way but be sure that the bird is very tender. For a little more thorough cooking, first brown on all sides, then drain off part of the fat, cover skillet and cook slowly for 35 to 40 minutes. A slightly different method suited to somewhat older chicken is to prepare as directed above, brown first, drain off fat, add a little water and cover closely, cooking slowly till tender.

—The Farmer's Wife Magazine

Select young spring chicken, about 2½ to 3 lbs. Dress and disjoint to prepare for pan. [*Editor's note*: wash in cold water and dry on paper towels 3 lbs. chicken pieces.] Chicken should be thoroughly chilled before it is used, several hours or overnight. To prepare for frying, sprinkle the slightly moist chicken with flour. Put just a few pieces at a time, so they do not touch, into a skillet containing hot fat fully 1½ inches deep. (in the Country Kitchen we used a full pound of fat in our large skillet and fried only six pieces at a time.) Fry gently, turning once. Each piece should be crusty brown on all sides, which is a characteristic of good southern fried chicken. Drain on paper towels or brown paper. In the South, peanut oil is used for frying; in the North, use lard or vegetable fat. After frying, strain fat into a can or a jar, where it can be used again and again if it is not overheated during use and if it is carefully strained after each using.

❧ Cream Gravy for Fried Chicken

1934

Remove chicken from pan when it is done; make gravy with some of the pan fat, flour, and milk. Use equal parts fat and flour, mix till smooth, then add hot milk, whisking all the while, until desired thickness. Season gravy with salt and paprika. Some cooks use as much as 1 tbsp. of paprika to make a rich-colored gravy.

❦ Chicken with Dumplings

February 1937

Stew chicken with onion in water to cover until almost done. Add salt and pepper, potato, and parsley. Boil 10 minutes, drop in dumplings (see below). Cover and cook 15 minutes without lifting the cover.

3½ lbs. chicken	3 tsp. baking powder
1 small onion, chopped	½ tsp. salt
salt and pepper to taste	1 tbsp. butter, plus extra for
1 large potato, peeled and diced	spreading over dough
¼ c. parsley, chopped	1 egg, beaten
2 c. sifted flour	about ½ c. milk

To make dumplings:

Sift together flour, baking powder, and salt. Rub in butter, add egg and milk to make a soft dough. Roll out on floured board, spread with butter, and sprinkle with pepper. Roll up like jelly roll and cut in rounds.

❦ Chicken Pie

November 1911

Take 3 pts. milk and 1 heaping tsp. salt, and sift in just enough flour to roll out but not a bit more. Line a deep dish on the bottom and sides with this pastry, letting it come well up over the edges of the pan all around. For filling, have ready two tender chickens that have been boiled in salted water till nearly tender, bones removed. Fill the pie with this chicken, dot bits of butter over the top, season to taste, then pour over the seasoned liquor in which the fowl has been boiled. Sift over a bit of flour, put on the top crust, in which large slits have been cut to let out the steam, and bake at 300°F for 2 hours.

🍂 Baking Powder Biscuits
March 1931

2 c. flour
4 tsp. baking powder
1 tsp. salt
4 tbsp. butter or shortening
¾ c. milk

Measure and sift the dry ingredients together; work in the butter or shortening either lightly with the fingertips or by cutting it in with two spatulas or knives. Add the milk all at once to the first mixture. Stir rapidly for a few seconds, turn out on a lightly floured board, knead vigorously about half a minute. Pat or roll to ½ inch or ¾ inch. Cut, transfer to a baking sheet (or to the top of a casserole), and bake at 400°F for 12 minutes.

🍂 Brunswick Stew
May 1936

Brunswick Stew in Virginia is as frequently made these modern times with a base of chicken, as it used to be made with a squirrel or a rabbit in pre-Revolutionary days. And it is as good as it is filling. Served with hot biscuits (see above) or better still, cornmeal spoon bread (pg. 74), you have a complete and satisfying meal.

—The Farmer's Wife Magazine

For a medium-sized chicken, dice ½ lb. salt pork or bacon and fry crisp in a deep stew pot. Add pieces of well-floured, boiled chicken and brown lightly. Pour in sufficient chicken broth to cover and add the following vegetables: 2 c. corn kernels, 2 c. lima or string beans, 1 c. tomato puree, 3 c. diced potatoes, and one large sliced onion. If available, add 1 c. sliced okra. Bring all to boil and simmer ½ hour, till all vegetables are tender. Then season with salt and pepper, thicken with flour, and serve all on a deep platter.

❦ Chicken Shortcake

April 1935
Contributed by M.C.P., New York

Muffins:

1 c. cornmeal	1 egg, beaten
1 c. flour	1 c. milk
3 tsp. baking powder	2 tbsp. melted butter
½ tsp. salt	

Mix and sift dry ingredients. Combine liquids and pour all at once into dry. Stir just to dampen. Fill large, greased muffin tins two-thirds full to make eight muffins. Bake at 425°F for 20 minutes.

Filling:

3 tbsp. butter	1 c. chicken stock
6 tbsp. flour	1½ c. diced cooked chicken
1 tsp. salt	8 pieces thinly sliced ham, cooked
2 c. milk	

Melt butter in double boiler, add flour and salt, and blend. Add milk and stock and stir till smooth. Add chicken and heat through. Split muffins, place a slice of cooked ham, lightly browned in butter, and a spoonful of chicken mixture on each, then put on top of muffin and another spoonful of chicken.

❦ Chicken Goulash

October 1929

1 whole chicken, 5–6 lbs.
2 c. tomatoes, chopped
2 tsp. salt
6 small onions, chopped
1 small green pepper, chopped

Boil chicken in water to cover till tender, about 2–2½ hours. When cool, remove the bones and cut the meat into small pieces. Return meat to broth, add remaining ingredients, and simmer 1 hour. Check seasoning before serving.

❦ Cuban Chicken

September 1928

1 chicken	1 clove
3 tbsp. butter	1 sprig parsley
2 onions, diced	3½ tsp. salt
2½ c. tomatoes, chopped	pepper to taste
1 c. water	1 c. rice, uncooked
1 green pepper, diced	1½ c. peas
1 tsp. paprika	1 chopped pimiento

Clean and cut chicken as for frying. Put butter in large pot and brown onions in it. Add tomatoes, water, green pepper, paprika, clove, parsley, salt, pepper, and chicken. Bring to a boil, cover, and continue to cook over low heat. Cook 1 hour, then add rice, peas, and pimiento; cover, bring to a boil again, then lower heat and simmer 1 more hour. Serve hot.

Chicken Casserole with Biscuits
September 1938

Cook a young fowl in water to cover until tender, adding a small onion, a stalk or two of celery, and 1 tbsp. salt while it is simmering. Remove meat from bones, leaving it in large, neat pieces. From the broth make gravy: first strain liquid, skim off fat and cook down, or add milk or water to make 4 c. of liquid. Thicken with ⅓ c. flour mixed with ¼ c. chicken fat (butter

may be used). Season, cook a few minutes. Put chicken pieces in casserole, adding enough hot gravy to cover. Put biscuits on top (see pg. 52) and bake 30 minutes in a hot oven (400°F). Chicken and gravy must be hot if biscuits are baked on top. Or, bake biscuits separately while chicken and gravy are heating in a covered casserole and put on top to serve. Serve extra gravy in a bowl.

Texas Hash
February 1921

2 c. rice
4 qts. boiling water
4 small onions, sliced
1 qt. tomatoes
2 tsp. salt
½ tsp. pepper
2 lbs. round steak, chopped fine

Cook rice in water over low flame till soft, then drain. Cook remaining ingredients together for 20 minutes. Add rice, put in buttered baking dish, and bake at 400°F for 15–20 minutes.

❦ Roast Beef Supreme

September 1937

Select two or three standing rib roasts. Wipe with a damp cloth and rub with salt and pepper. Place the roast in a dripping pan with the fat side up. Do not cover the roast and do not add any water. Place the meat in a slow oven (300°F) and roast to the desired degree of doneness. A meat thermometer will register 140°F for a rare roast, 160°F for a medium roast, and 170°F for a well-done roast. Allow 18 to 20 minutes to the pound for cooking a rare roast, 22 to 25 minutes to the pound for medium, and 27 to 30 minutes to the pound for a well-done roast. A 4-lb. roast will serve six to eight people.

❦ Beef Cakes with Brown Gravy

July–August 1921

This recipe may be of assistance to someone who is tired of "the same old things" for the hungry, once-a-year gang of men who come to thresh.
                                        —The Farmer's Wife Magazine

Prepare beef cakes from ground beef that contains plenty of fat. Brown on both sides in a hot skillet, and when a sufficient number of cakes are browned, remove and drain on paper towels and make a gravy by adding 1 c. hot water, salt and pepper to taste, and 1 tbsp. flour to the skillet. When thickened, pour gravy over the cakes, season again with salt and pepper, put in the oven, and cook ½ hour at 350°F. Serve meat and gravy on a platter together.

Broiled Hamburgers
November 1938

2 large, mild onions	1 c. soft breadcrumbs
3 tbsp. butter	1 tbsp. parsley, chopped
1 tbsp. water	2 tsp. Onion Juice (see below)
1 lb. lean ground beef	salt and pepper
¼ c. ground suet or butter	7 bacon strips

Cut onions into seven ½-inch slices. Place flat in baking dish, add butter and water, and cover closely. Bake at 350°F. Meanwhile, mix other ingredients except bacon, then knead into seven flat cakes. Wrap each cake with a bacon strip and place on slice of onion. Broil under direct heat, 5 minutes for each side, basting occasionally.

Onion Juice:
Peel and grate an onion. Strain through a sieve and store reserved juice in a covered jar in the refrigerator.

Variation:
Cook on top of the stove, with sliced mushrooms sautéed in butter in place of onion.

"THOSE AWFUL THRESHERS"
The True Story of How One Prairie Wife Fed 'Em
August 1919
Pearl Riggs Crouch

The hush of sunset was upon the prairie. The afterglow was kindling to rose the reaches of the sky. Against the vivid back-drop of the west, a vast bulk lurched over the limestone hill, and slowly a fluted banner of smudgy smoke unfurled.

Puff—puff—nearer, clearer came a summons unmistakable, imperative. It was to be my privilege to play, tomorrow, the generous— yet *à la Hoover*—hostess to a dozen husky creatures who, with contempt for apology, exalted the pleasures of the palate!

I had not expected them quite yet—of course not! Had I not been warned for a year that they would come like a gust of wind around the corner? Could I turn the trick, alone?

I bolted blithely into my workshop to set the ball a-rolling.

But it was a full five minutes before my gyrating mind could manage a menu: pinto beans, the inevitable pièce de résistance of the threshers' daily banquet; mashed spuds; cabbage and ham; sliced tomato pickles; rice pudding with raisins; cranberry jelly; homemade bread and butter.

I plunged into the meal bin after the beans, lately threshed, and washed and put to soak nearly a gallon; started the water to boiling for the rice; made a perilous trip down the half-finished cellar-way for cabbage and settled myself to cutting.

The next morning about five-thirty, I was rudely snatched from sleep by a fierce, intermittent snorting, and recalled in a flash my husband's warning: "They'll be out early to get up steam, possibly threshing by seven-thirty."

Breakfast over and morning cleaning out of the way, my operations began. I drained the soaked beans and put them on; mixed the raisins, fattened by brief boiling, with the beaten eggs, milk, and drained rice; added the jelly and popped the pudding onto the oven; started the ham and cabbage. Then I sat down on my white enameled stool to peel a peck of spuds. Half an hour later I put them to boil. While things were merrily cooking, I set to work arranging my table.

We had fixed the tiny kitchen porch for the men's washing and combing. When they began to lunge in—big, smiling fellows, faces beaming from hasty application of soap, water, and a rough towel, hair

a but ruffled from brief brushing, stepping lightly as if fearing to crush something delicate in my little white kitchen, I felt suddenly composed. I smiled back and piloted them to the dining table.

The beans proved the most popular dish, with cranberry jelly a close second. In twenty minutes it was all over, and alone, I faced the table. It did not look as it had half an hour before!

❦ Chili
October 1938

3 lbs. ground beef
3 onions
1 c. flour blended into 1 c. hot butter and browned
32 oz. thick tomato puree
3 lbs. cooked red beans
¾ lb. cooked spaghetti
salt and pepper to taste

Beef and onions are browned in fat; add tomato and beans and cook till thick. Season with salt and pepper, adding spaghetti just before serving to heat through.

❦ Pot Roast and Noodles
June 1930

Use the large pieces of beef, such as the ribs. Melt a little fat in a kettle and brown the meat well on all sides. Add water to cover and cook until tender. In the meantime, cook broad noodles until tender in boiling, salted water. Drain and add a little liquor—about ½ c.—from the cooked meat. Simmer until the noodles have become well flavored with the meat juices. Serve in a border around the meat.

❦ Meat Loaf

March 1922

1 lb. lean ground pork
2 lbs. ground beef
½ small onion, chopped
½ loaf stale bread, crumbed
2 eggs, slightly beaten
1 c. milk
1 tsp. salt
¼ tsp. pepper
3 strips bacon

Add all ingredients but bacon together and form into a loaf. Place in well-greased loaf pan, packing entirely to fill the corners. Place bacon strips on top and bake 2 hours at 350°F.

❦ Loose Meat Sandwiches

October 1938
Also known these days as Sloppy Joes.

3 lbs. ground lean beef
⅓ c. fat
2 c. green tomatoes, diced
¼ c. onion, finely chopped
¼ c. celery, finely chopped
1 tbsp. salt
buns
butter

Cook ground beef in hot fat until lightly browned. Add vegetables and seasoning. Let simmer until well-cooked and slightly thick. Split buns, toast, and butter. Spread with hot mixture and serve.

❧ Beef Stew
January 1924

4 tbsp. butter
2 lbs. beef
2 c. carrots, chopped
2 onions, thinly sliced
8 medium-sized potatoes, cut in cubes
4 tbsp. flour
4 tbsp. milk or water

Heat butter in kettle. Cut meat in small pieces and brown in butter. Add enough water to cook meat and vegetables. Add carrots and onions when meat has cooked ½ hour. Add potatoes ½ hour before stew is done (usually 3 hours). Make a paste of the flour and an equal amount of cold water or milk. Add enough more cold liquid so the paste will pour. Add to stew and cook 5 minutes to thicken. Cooked rice, macaroni or hominy, cabbage, tomatoes, peas, beans, okra, and turnips may be added. Parsley, celery tops, or chopped sweet peppers add to flavor. To thicken stews allow 2 tbsp. flour to each pint of water used in making the stew.

❧ Curried Brisket with Rice Border
November 1917

2 lbs. beef brisket   2 tbsp. flour
2 c. onion, cut fine   2 tsp. curry powder
2 tsp. salt   1 tbsp. celery, chopped

Wipe the meat and cut in narrow strips. Sear on both sides in hot frying pan, then put in large stew kettle and cover with boiling water. Brown the onions in the pan where the meat was seared and add them to the meat. Season and simmer 3 hours or till tender. Mix flour and curry powder with a little cold water, add to meat, and also the celery. Boil 10–15 minutes. When celery is tender, turn onto a platter, surround with a border of cooked rice, and serve.

❦ Pork-and-Bean Pie with Sweet Potato Topping

March 1943

Meat-extending dishes are easy to prepare and usually more healthful than so many fried steaks and chops. Good meat flavor goes a long way in gravies, stews, sauces, or in combination dishes, where the filler is potatoes, bread, macaroni, dried beans, or rice.

—The Farmer's Wife Magazine

2 c. seasoned baked beans
1 c. pork cubes, browned and cooked on the stove top for several minutes
2 c. sweet potatoes, roasted and mashed
Pork stock or liquid to moisten

Combine pork and beans and arrange in casserole. Top with a ring of sweet potato. Bake until heated through and browned, about ½ hour at 350°F.

❦ Pork Chop Casserole

June 1927

6 pork chops
½ c. uncooked rice, rinsed
1 28-oz can tomatoes
1 small onion, chopped
salt and pepper to taste

Place pork chops in baking dish. Add rice, tomato, and chopped onion as you want. Season with salt and pepper and cover with water. Bake at 350°F for 2 hours.

❦ Stuffed Pork Tenderloin
1934

2 lbs. pork tenderloin
Sage Stuffing (see below)
2 tbsp. pickles, chopped
flour
salt and pepper to taste

Split tenderloin in half lengthwise, leaving halves joined together. Pound slightly. Fill with stuffing and pickles. Fold meat halves together and tie with twine. Sprinkle with flour, salt, and pepper. Roast at 350°F for 1 hour, basting occasionally.

❦ Sage Stuffing
November 1914

Soak a little more than 1 pt. breadcrumbs in 1 c. well-seasoned beef or chicken stock. Add 1 tbsp. powdered sage, a little more salt and pepper if necessary, and one small onion, finely chopped. Add enough melted butter or sweet cream to moisten and mix in two unbeaten eggs.

❧ Roast Stuffed Spareribs
December 1934

2 sides of spareribs
¼ c. butter
1 onion, chopped
1 pt. soft breadcrumbs
1 pt. cold cooked potatoes, chopped
1 tsp. powdered sage
2 tsp. salt
1 tsp. pepper
salt, pepper, flour

Trim spareribs so they make two neat, rectangular pieces. Wipe with a damp cloth. Sprinkle with salt and pepper and sew together on one side, using a darning needle and some string. Melt 2 tbsp. butter in a skillet, add onion, then breadcrumbs and potatoes. Cook until lightly browned and heated through (no moisture other than the potatoes is needed). Add sage, salt, and pepper; pile lightly on one rib section and sew on the other side. Rub with seasoned flour. Place on a rack over a dripping pan or a roasting pan. Bake uncovered at 450°F for the first 20 minutes, then at 375°F until well done, about an hour longer. Serve on a platter with glazed onions and baked apples. To serve, carve between ribs.

❦ Baked Southampton Ham

March 1938

Virginia hams are given a longer, more peppery cure than northern hams. Both flavor and texture are different—the fat is softer since hogs are fattened on peanuts and field peas; the flavor is much stronger than northern hams.

—The Farmer's Wife Magazine

These days it is virtually impossible to procure a raw ham like the one described below (unless you happen to be a pig farmer, or know one). Your butcher or supermarket meat section will likely offer a fully cooked bone-in ham, in which case you should proceed with the following recipe beginning with the instructions for studding the ham with cloves.

Cut off long shank end if ham is to be served whole; scrub thoroughly. Soak overnight and put skin side down in boiler, adding fresh cold water to cover. Let come to boiling point and simmer slowly, allowing 20–25 minutes per pound from time it reaches simmering boil. Add hot water as needed to keep ham covered. When done, take ham from boiler and remove skin while warm, trimming off excess fat to give the ham a neat appearance. (Some cooks let the ham cool in its liquor and then trim.) Dot the back with cloves, then sprinkle with brown sugar and cracker crumbs, mixed. Bake in oven at 350°F till brown. To carve, begin about 2½ inches from hock end, on back of the ham. Make first cut straight to bone, then cut off ⅛-inch slices with knife at angle of 45 degrees.

❦ Ham and Sour Cream Casserole
May 1933

2½ c. noodles
3 qts. water
1 tsp. salt
1 small onion, chopped
2 tsp. parsley, chopped
3 tbsp. butter
1 lb. cooked ham, cut in small pieces
3 eggs, beaten
½ tsp. nutmeg
⅛ tsp. pepper
2 c. sour cream
1 c. breadcrumbs

Boil the noodles until tender in salted water. Drain and set aside. Brown the onion and parsley in the butter. Add the ham and remove from the stove. Beat together the eggs, nutmeg, pepper, and sour cream and add to the ham. Add the drained noodles and mix. Place in a greased baking dish and spread the breadcrumbs on top. Bake uncovered for 30 minutes at 350°F or until set.

❦ Ham Succotash in Casserole
July 1938

3 c. corn kernels
3 c. fresh or frozen lima beans
1 tbsp. minced onion
2 c. cooked ham, cut in strips
2 tbsp. butter
2½ c. milk

Simmer corn and limas in water to cover, along with onion, for 10 minutes. Fry ham in butter and put in bottom of baking dish. Pour vegetables and milk over it. Bake at 350°F for 30 minutes.

Escalloped Ham and Potatoes
February 1923

6 medium-sized potatoes
2 thick slices raw ham
2 tbsp. flour
¼ tsp. pepper (optional)
2 c. milk

Pare and cut potatoes into thin slices. Dredge the slices of ham with flour and arrange potatoes and ham in alternate layers in a baking dish, placing one slice of ham on top. Pour on milk sufficient to reach to the top slice of ham. Bake at 375°F for 45 minutes, or until the ham is tender. Pepper, if used, should be sprinkled between layers of ham and potato. Because of the salt in the ham, added salt will not be necessary. Serve from the baking dish.

Macaroni with Minced Ham
September 1919

2 c. cooked macaroni
2 c. minced ham
2 c. creamed corn
1 c. breadcrumbs
butter
salt and pepper to taste

Arrange macaroni, ham, and corn in alternate layers in a buttered baking dish. Cover with crumbs and dot with butter. Bake at 400°F till brown. Always remember that ham is salt.

❧ Schnitz un Knepp

February 1937
A Pennsylvania Dutch dish.

1 pt. dried sweet apples
2 to 4 lbs. shank end of ham
Dumplings (see below)
2 tbsp. brown sugar
flour and water paste

Soak apples (*schnitz*) in water to cover; let stand on back of stove about 3 hours. Simmer ham till almost done, add apples, drained of part of juice, and boil ½ hour longer. Add Dumplings (*knepp*, see below) and cook 15 minutes. When done, place dumplings on a large platter around the ham, cut in serving pieces. Baking powder or raised dumplings may be used, but Miss Cole says they like raised dumplings best.

Raised Dumplings (Knepp):
¾ c. milk
About 3¼ c. sifted flour
1 tbsp. sugar
pinch salt

Scald milk, cool to lukewarm, and add 1 c. flour, sugar, and salt. Let raise till spongy, then add the rest of the flour or enough to make a dough to handle. Make into twelve dumplings like you make rolls, put on greased tin, and let raise till light. Drop into kettle of boiling broth and meat (see Schnitz, above). Cover and cook 15 minutes.

❦ Sausage Pudding
April 1935

1 c. cooked oatmeal	½ tsp. salt
1 c. milk	2 tsp. baking powder
2 eggs, separated	12 sausage links
1 c. flour	

Blend oatmeal with milk and yolks. Sift in dry ingredients, beat well, and fold in stiffly beaten egg whites. Pour into shallow, buttered baking pan and lay sausage links across. Bake at 400°F about 25 minutes, till firm and beginning to brown. Remove and pour off fat. Return to oven and bake 5 minutes longer, till well browned. Drain off fat again. Serve hot, plain or with a gravy made of 3 tbsp. sausage fat, 4 tbsp. flour, 2 c. milk, and ½ tsp. salt.

■■■

❦ Pepper Pot
October 1928
A Pennsylvania Dutch recipe.

Put a knuckle of veal into a pot with 2½ lbs. diced stewed tripe. Cover with 3 qts. cold water, pepper and salt, a bunch of parsley, and 1 tbsp. chopped sweet marjoram. Cook 4 hours, then add two large potatoes cut in cubes. Cover and cook ½ hour. Add small Bread Dumplings (below). Lift the stew and thicken the gravy with 1 heaping tbsp. flour mixed with water.

Brood Khutjes (Bread Dumplings):
Soak 3 slices white bread in 1 c. broth, squeeze dry, and beat smooth with a fork. Heat 1 tbsp. butter and put in the bread, adding pepper and salt. When cool, add 1 tbsp. chopped parsley, a little grated nutmeg, two beaten eggs, and enough flour to bind. Form in small balls, roll in flour, and poach 3 minutes in stew.

❦ Lamb Stew
September 1937

2 lbs. veal or lean lamb shoulder
3 tbsp. lard
3 c. boiling water
4 carrots
1 small stalk celery
6 small white onions, peeled
6 medium-sized potatoes
1 ½ tsp. salt
pepper to taste
2 tbsp. chopped parsley

Wipe the meat with a damp cloth. Cut into 2-inch cubes. Brown well in a kettle containing hot lard. Add boiling water, cover, and simmer for 45 minutes. Add the vegetables: the carrots cut in lengthwise pieces, the celery in 4-inch sticks, the onions whole, and the potatoes in halves. Add salt and pepper and cook for 45 minutes more. When all are done, remove to a hot platter, piling the meat cubes in the center and arranging the vegetables in separate piles around the edge of the platter. Sprinkle meat with chopped parsley. Thicken gravy with flour, if desired; serve in separate bowl.

❦ Gravy
April 1925

If you have cooked any sort of meat in a pan or skillet, you can make gravy from the drippings. Otherwise, a simple gravy can be made by following instructions for White Sauce (pg. 89), substituting broth for milk. Stir until thick and season with salt and pepper.

❦ Frankfurter Crown, Potato Dressing
September 1937

1 ½ lbs. frankfurters
Potato Dressing (see below)
3 slices bacon

Thread frankfurters through center on a string, tie ends of string, and stand frankfurters on end in shape of a crown on rack in a roasting pan. Fill center with potato dressing. Place slices of bacon on top of dressing. Bake at 350°F until bacon browns. Add ½ c. water, cover, and let cook 20 minutes.

Potato Dressing:
4 slices bacon
1 tbsp. onion, chopped
1 tbsp. parsley, chopped
1 tsp. salt
⅛ tsp. pepper
1 qt. bread cubes
1 egg, slightly beaten
2 c. mashed potatoes

Dice bacon and brown. Add onion and cook slowly till tender. Add seasonings. Combine with bread, then add slightly beaten egg and mashed potatoes. Toss together till evenly combined. Add water till mixture is of desired consistency.

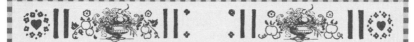

WHEN YOU FEED THE
THRESHING CREW
August 1923

Mrs. Mark Kroxell

The threshers were to be at Fair Oaks Farm on Wednesday. For weeks, in fact nearly ever since their last visit, Mrs. Thurston had known just what her menus were to be, and she knew the importance of having her every part—but especially HER part—of the threshing, a success. With the washing and ironing out of the way, nothing remained but the cooking and the last-minute details. Mrs. Briggs, her nearest neighbor, was coming over to help with the food which was to be prepared on Tuesday, and some of the others in the neighborhood would be there early Wednesday to assist. All of them knew that Mrs. Thurston was going to try a cafeteria, and they were as excited and expectant as the Thurston children.

Wednesday dawned bright and fair. Dinner was to be the first meal served, and as the men were expected to finish by suppertime on Thursday night, preparations were made for five meals, with reserves on hand in case a breakdown or accident delayed the work.

Noon found the dining room wearing an entirely new aspect from the usual. The table was stretched out to its greatest capacity, and along the side, next to the door opening into the kitchen, was a long counter covered with white oilcloth on which were placed all the articles needed for serving. The main part of the cooking was done on the trusty old coal range in the kitchen, but the oil stove was moved into the dining room behind the counter for preparation of the coffee and to keep things hot. A porch at the back of the house provided a wash room for the men. There was a pump beside it, towels hung on the adjacent rack, and a bench supplied with basins and soap for their use. In gaining her husband's consent to try the plan, Mrs. Thurston had also enlisted his cooperation. He wanted it to be a success and, after it was finally decided upon, became as enthusiastic as his wife. He jovially directed the men, "Right here at this end, boys. Get a tray and help yourselves. Take some of everything and come back as often as you like. We're going to train you up in city styles."

As fast as the men filled their trays they passed on, some out of doors, some around the dining table, and some out on the porch. They gathered in groups and talked over the morning's work. They relaxed and laughed

and had ten times as much fun as they could have had if half a dozen women had been waiting on them.

Every meal during the threshing was served the same way, and when the crew left, the boss told Mrs. Thurston that her meals were more satisfactory to the men than any they had had that season. Best of all, she herself went to the Ladies' Aid the next day feeling as fit as ever, instead of ready for a sanitarium. By the use of a little ingenious planning, her work had been cut almost in half, and she knew that threshing would hold no more terrors for her in the future.

Original Salmon and Potato Loaf with Mushroom Sauce

June 1934
Contributed by Mrs. G.A.C., Louisiana

3 c. mashed potatoes
1 15-oz. can salmon, flaked
½ c. grated cheddar cheese
1 tsp. Onion Juice (pg. 57)

1 tsp. lemon juice
½ tsp. salt
⅛ tsp. pepper

Mix in order given and press into buttered casserole. Bake 30 minutes at 350°F, unmold on a platter, and surround with:

Mushroom Sauce:
Brown ¼ c. butter, then add 1 c. sliced mushrooms and 4 tbsp. flour. Stir till flour browns, add 2 c. milk, and cook 20 minutes over low flame. Season to taste.

Note from Farmer's Wife *editor:* Light and fluffy; well-seasoned; really delicious. I used hot mashed potatoes. If you use leftovers, add hot milk and a little baking powder to liven them up.

Side Dishes

Miss Linda's Hoecakes

January 1921

Sift together 1½ c. cornmeal, 1 tsp. salt, and 2 tsp. baking powder. Beat the yolks of two eggs till light, then add 1 c. milk and beat into the meal. Fold in the beaten egg whites and shape the dough into oblong shapes upon a well-greased griddle. Cook over medium heat till golden; flip and cook second side till golden and hoecake is hot through.

Cornmeal Spoon Bread

October 1923

2 c. cornmeal
1 tbsp. sugar
1 tsp. salt
2 tsp. baking soda
4 c. sour milk
1 egg
1 tbsp. fat

Sift dry ingredients together, add milk gradually, drop in egg, add fat, and beat mixture thoroughly. Bake in greased baking dish at 375°F for 30–45 minutes, depending upon size and depth of pan.

❦ Corn Bread
March 1921

1 c. fine cornmeal
1 c. flour
1 tbsp. sugar
1 tsp. baking soda
1 tsp. salt
1 tbsp. shortening
Milk or buttermilk, as indicated below
1 egg, well beaten

Sift dry ingredients together. Then work in 1 tablespoonful shortening. Mix to a medium batter with milk or buttermilk. Whip in one well-beaten egg and bake at 400°F for about 20 minutes, till cooked through.

❦ Baked Hominy and Cheese
October 1933
Contributed by Iowa State College

1 15-oz. can hominy, drained
½ to 1 c. grated cheddar cheese
pepper
1 c. milk
1 tbsp. flour
1 tbsp. butter

Place in buttered baking dish, alternating layers of hominy and cheese. Season with salt and pepper. Pour over White Sauce made with milk, butter, and flour (pg. 89). Dot with butter and bake at 350°F for 25 minutes, till golden and bubbling.

Knedliky (Bohemian)

February 1928
Contributed by Mrs. M.V., Ohio

4 c. flour
1¾ c. milk
1 egg
1 tbsp. salt
½ tsp. baking powder
2 slices bacon, chopped
½ an onion, sliced

Mix together making a stiff dough that will hold the spoon upright. Have water boiling and dip the spoon first in the boiling water; then, take a spoonful of the dough and drop into the boiling water. When all the dough has been dipped in water, cover and let boil for 5 minutes, then stir from the bottom. Replace the cover and boil for 25 minutes. Remove one dumpling from kettle to see if it is done on the inside. If not, let them boil longer. Drain and place in a bowl. In a skillet, fry some bacon and onion and pour over the bowl of knedliky. Serve at once.

Potato Knedliky (Bohemian)

February 1928
Contributed by Mrs. M.V., Ohio

4 c. flour
1 tbsp. salt
2 c. mashed potatoes
1½ c. milk

Mix into a very stiff dough and boil the same as the other kind (see Knedliky, above). Never use baking powder with knedliky, and do not let them boil too long or they will dissolve.

❧ Oven Fried Potatoes
May 1934

Pare potatoes and cut lengthwise in strips as for French fries. Let stand in cold water 15 or 20 minutes while oven is getting hot (400°F). Melt butter or bacon fat in a flat, fairly shallow baking dish, about 1 tbsp. to a potato. Drain potatoes thoroughly, stir in the fat until they are coated, and sprinkle with salt and pepper. Bake at 400°F, allowing up to 45 minutes to brown. Stir once.

❧ Potato Cakes
February 1937

2 c. cold mashed potatoes
2 eggs
¼ c. flour
¼ tsp. salt
2 tbsp. milk
1 small onion, minced
1 tbsp. parsley, minced

Mix all ingredients, drop with spoon in hot fat in frying pan, and flatten. Fry on both sides till brown.

❦ Scalloped Potatoes
November 1922

7 lbs. potatoes
salt and pepper
½ c. flour
½ lb. butter
2–4 c. milk, scalded

Wash, pare, soak, and cut potatoes in ¼-inch slices. Put a layer in buttered baking dishes (you will probably need two) or shallow pans, sprinkle with salt and pepper, dredge with flour, and dot with butter. Repeat till pans are filled. Add hot milk to reach up to the top layer of potatoes. Bake gently at 375°F till potatoes are soft and golden.

❦ Escalloped Potatoes in Tomato Sauce
May 1933

1¼ c. peeled, sliced potatoes
2–3 onions, peeled and sliced
1½ tsp. salt
½ tsp. pepper
2 tbsp. flour
2 c. strained or crushed tomatoes
2 tbsp. butter

Put layer of potatoes in buttered baking dish, and sprinkle with onion, seasoning, and flour; repeat till potatoes are used up. Add tomatoes, dot with butter, cover, and bake at 375°F till done, 1 to 1½ hours.

❧ Potato Pancakes I
May 1918

6 large raw potatoes, grated
1½ tsp. salt
1 tbsp. milk
1 egg, beaten
3 tbsp. flour

Mix above ingredients, beat thoroughly, and cook on both sides on a hot griddle in oil or butter, flipping once.

❧ Potato Pancakes II
May 1918

1 c. boiled potatoes, mashed or ground in a ricer
½ tsp. salt
1 egg, beaten
¼ c. milk

Mix ingredients in order given, beat thoroughly, and cook as above.

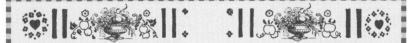

HARVEST TIME MEALS AS PLANNED BY FARM HOMEMAKERS IN 35 STATES

July 1935

I have just finished a "journey" to 35 states to see how farm homemakers plan and serve harvest-time meals. My "trip" took me from Maine to Oregon, and from Texas to Tennessee to Ontario, Canada. My "journey," of course, was by the letter route. In March we asked our readers to send us menus and recipes for their best harvest-time meals, and a huge box of replies came. What fun it was to read them, for those letters made me feel as though I were actually visiting in farm homes. And now I share my profitable experiences with all of you who are interested in the problem of harvest-time cookery.

—Miriam J. Williams

Yes, there are traditions when it comes to harvest meals. The theme is unmistakable: *Hungry men do not care for fancy dishes. They want plenty of good food, well cooked.* And I'm sure they're getting it in most communities, to judge from the contest letters. Many a woman said that hard-working men deserve good meals and that she enjoyed providing them. Even though many wrote of cooking and serving a crew unaided, there was no hint of complaint of hard work, only of satisfaction of a task well done.

With a few rare exceptions, dinners and suppers were built around a hearty meat dish. Meat loaf headed the list, with roast beef next. Other favorites were: baked or boiled ham, fried and stewed chicken, browned home-canned meat, roast pork, steak—smothered or Swiss-style—chicken, or meat pie. Interesting "strays" were barbecued ribs, pork chops en casserole, baked domestic rabbit, mulligan and Brunswick stew, meatballs, fried ham and cream gravy, corned beef, chop suey, casserole of sausage, and many combination dishes.

Potatoes? *Of course!* Three times a day in some cases where a hearty breakfast was served. And the men want them mashed. No other single dish chalked up a score like mashed potatoes, unless it was gravy or bread and butter, of course. Boiled or browned potatoes were popular with roast dinners where there was plenty of good brown gravy. Scalloped potatoes were a prime favorite with meat loaf and ham dinners, or with cold, sliced meats served for supper. It almost amounts to a law—don't forget potatoes.

As for other vegetables, no one could be more surprised than I was at the variety that men eat—carrots, alone and in combination with cabbage, with celery, or with peas; Harvard-style beets and beet greens; turnips, scalloped and creamed with peas; summer squash; sauerkraut; green limas, spinach with egg slices; stewed tomatoes and green corn; creamed onions; savory mixed vegetables; broccoli. You can guess the favorites—beans, both green and baked dried beans; corn; peas; tomatoes; cabbage; cucumbers and lettuce. And when I began a list of different kinds of salad served, my skepticism, born of "harvest men don't eat salads," began to disappear. While nothing could get ahead of crisp cabbage slaw, yet the other salads must have been popular to judge from the number a recipe would serve.

The bread was mostly homemade in the form of plain and fancy rolls, dark and light sliced bread, steamed brown bread, cornbread, biscuits, and occasionally, muffins. A few mentioned buying sliced bread in town. Rolls were often baked the day before, or early in the day, to be reheated in a covered pan or paper sack before serving. Jelly or preserves of some kind usually accompanied bread and butter.

Coffee, iced tea, cold fruit drinks, and buttermilk were the accepted drinks. When it came to the drink taken to the field, it frequently was hot coffee if a lunch was served, and cold buttermilk or lemonade if sent out alone. You can guess the most popular dessert—pie, and apple pie at that. There were variations, however—apple pie with cheese crust, deep-dish apple pie with its thick, flaky crust on top, and the open-faced kind with crust beneath and cream on top. Lemon pie and sour-cream raisin pie ranked high in popularity, with chocolate, custard, and berry pies next in line. Canned or fresh fruit, served both as "sauce" or in a quivery jelly, and flanked with cake or cookies, was second to pie in popularity. Spicy cakes and cookies seem to be men's favorites, for they represented nearly 50 percent of the ninety-two cake and cookie recipes submitted. And next in number came chocolate cakes— many of these made with sour cream as a time-saving feature.

There was a surprisingly wide range of puddings and cobblers. I liked these particularly: fresh peach cobbler, Dutch apple cake with caramel sauce, a creamy rice pudding served with maple syrup from Vermont, a cocoanut-sweet potato pudding from North Carolina, spiced baked apples served with cream and a plate of creole chocolate cake, a fruited tapioca which could be made ahead, and a generous shortcake from Kansas calling for a *gallon* of strawberries! Homemade ice cream was looked upon as the dessert supreme, sometimes served at the last meal as a special treat.

How much do harvesters eat? Plenty of what you serve is the cue, and 486 quantity recipes submitted bear this out. A city meat loaf in my file calls for 6 lbs. of meat for twenty-five people, while the recipes submitted in this contest average 8 to 10 lbs. of meat for twenty-five servings. For baked beans, bring out the biggest crocks for harvest season. The good cooks do not agree, but it seems to take from 2 to 3 qts. dry beans to serve twenty-five. For eight men, says a neatly written recipe for Green Beans, Southern-Style, use 1 *gallon* green beans. Another for scalloped corn suggests 4 c. for eight servings. Two pies will serve eight, says one lady; others think ten. A recipe for pineapple ice cream goes like this: 3¹/₂ qts. milk, 14 eggs, 1 can crushed pineapple, 1 qt. cream, with sugar and salt, of course. It ended up, "This will make 2 gallons and will serve twenty to thirty portions." Perhaps—just perhaps, the family was extra.

❦ Norwegian Cloob or Potato Dumplings

February 1928
Contributed by Mrs. F.M. D.W., South Dakota

1 dozen medium-sized potatoes, cooked and mashed
1 dozen medium-sized potatoes, grated
3 eggs, beaten
1 tsp. salt
3 tbsp. milk

Mix together and knead stiff like bread. Wet hands with water and knead balls with a small piece of pork fat in center. Boil in pork or chicken broth for 1 hour; drain and serve with butter.

❦ Baked Rice

November 1931

2 c. uncooked rice, rinsed
3½ c. meat stock
3–4 slices bacon
1 onion, sliced

1 tbsp. green pepper, minced
¾ c. tomato sauce, seasoned
salt and pepper to taste

Add rice gradually to the boiling stock. Place over hot water and steam 20 minutes, or till stock is absorbed. Brown bacon slightly and remove to another pan. Cook onion and pepper in bacon fat till browned. Add rice and mix well. Add tomato sauce. Cover with slices of bacon. Brown at 450°F.

❦ Boston Baked Beans
February 1935

1 qt. dried navy, pinto, or small white beans
1 small onion, peeled and chopped
¼ lb. salt pork or bacon
½ to 1 tbsp. salt
½ tbsp. prepared mustard
1 c. hot water
3 tbsp. molasses

Wash and soak beans in cold water to cover overnight. In the morning, drain, cover with fresh water, and cook slowly until the skins break—45–50 minutes. Drain. Place onion in bottom of earthenware bean pot; pour in beans. Score rind of salt pork (or chop bacon). Mix seasonings and hot water together. Bury pork in beans, leaving rind exposed (or mix in chopped bacon). Add molasses and hot water mixture. Cover bean pot and bake in a slow oven (250°F) 6 to 8 hours. Add water as necessary. Bake uncovered the last hour.

❧ Corn and Pepper Sauté
September 1938

Cook lightly in butter one shredded sweet red pepper and one green pepper. When soft but not brown, add 4 c. corn kernels. Season with salt and paprika. Heat thoroughly and serve.

❧ Creole Green Corn
October 1920

6 ears fresh corn
1 tbsp. oil or butter
1 sweet red pepper, chopped

Cut the corn from the cob and put in the frying pan with the fat. Cook 10 minutes, then add the chopped pepper and season with salt. (A small, minced onion may be added, and two ripe tomatoes.)

SPRING FOOD-TONICS
Cooling Foods
May 1920
Lucy D. Cordiner

The idea of coolness is given by the color green. Actual resistance to the effect of hot weather is possible when green vegetables enter into the summer dietary. Wild greens, such as dandelions, cowslips, dock or pigweed, and the cultivated spinach, Swiss chard, beet tops, lettuces, and asparagus are the friends of man, as indeed are all the summer vegetables, radishes, onions, tomatoes, and the fruits, remarkable for their cooling acid properties.

The products of the garden should appear on the table for breakfast, dinner, and supper. Children should be required to use them freely. Adults who do not use them earn their punishment.

The greens I have mentioned may be cooked in the simplest way. Pick them over carefully and discard all yellow or withered leaves. Wash in several waters to remove sand or grit. These vegetables give up their juices when cooking and therefore should not be cooked in a large quantity of water. Put into the kettle just enough water to prevent burning. Add the greens, cover and let simmer for half an hour, then lift the cover and let the liquor boil down. [*Editor's note*: a quick sauté in a skillet with a little olive oil and a few tablespoons of water is a quicker, healthier, and more up-to-date method for cooking most greens.] When the greens are tender drain them, and use the liquor as the basis for any kind of sauce to be served as an accompaniment. If the vegetable is to be served simply with butter, salt, and pepper, use the liquor in soup. It is too valuable to throw away as it usually contains the dissolved minerals which make vegetables such cooling foods.

There are at least six ways in which greens may be served:

1. With salt, pepper, and butter
2. Garnish with hard-boiled eggs; put the yolks through the vegetable ricer and cut the whites into rings; serve as in 1.
3. Serve with a white sauce, made with ½ c. liquor, ½ c. milk, 1 tbsp. butter, 1 tbsp. flour
4. Serve with any well-liked salad dressing
5. Serve on toast garnished with strips of pimiento

❧ Lima Beans in Casserole
July 1929

¼ lb. chopped bacon
2 onions, sliced
2 c. fresh shelled lima beans, parboiled 2 minutes
1 c. milk
1 tsp. salt
½ tsp. pepper

Brown the bacon, remove to drain and cook the sliced onions in remaining fat till tender. Combine all ingredients, place in a greased casserole and bake at 325°F till beans are very tender. More milk may be needed—add to casserole ¼ c. at a time, as necessary.

❧ Spanish Lima Beans
May 1938

1½ c. lima beans, shelled
2 tbsp. butter
2 tbsp. onion, chopped
1½ c. tomatoes, diced
sugar, salt, pepper to taste
½ c. fine breadcrumbs

Boil lima beans in lightly salted water till just tender—10–20 minutes. Drain. Cook onion in butter till soft, then add tomatoes and seasonings. Simmer 10 minutes, then add lima beans and crumbs till hot through. Serve immediately.

❧ Baked Onions
July–August 1921

Prepare onions of medium size by peeling. Boil 15 minutes in salted water, drain, place in a baking dish, add whole milk to come well up around the onions but not to cover them, season with salt and pepper, and bake slowly at 300°F till they can be pierced with a toothpick. Serve hot.

❧ French Fried Onions
March 1933

Cut peeled yellow onions into ¼-inch slices. Separate into rings. Dip in milk and flour seasoned with salt and pepper. Fry in deep, hot fat till golden brown. Drain on paper towels or brown paper and sprinkle with salt. Serve immediately.

❧ Creamed Onion Tops
April 1926

3 bunches young onions
3 tbsp. butter
3 tbsp. flour
2 c. milk
½ tsp. salt
pepper

Cut onion tops into pieces and cook with onions in plenty of boiling, salted water. Melt butter, blend with flour, add milk, salt, and pepper to taste. Stir till thick, boil 1 minute, and serve over drained greens.

❦ Peas
May 1936

Of course we all agree that to do anything to peas other than boil them quickly for 15 minutes, season with salt and pepper, and liberally douse with butter is an emergency measure. But take a tip from the frugal French women and when more people come than there are peas to serve  them, add an equal amount of slivered lettuce to the peas. Boil as usual, with the addition of one small onion, minced. Drain and serve with a thin White Sauce (see below). Don't be afraid to try this, for it is really delicious, and like anything in white sauce, it is a great little old appeaser for the appetite.

❦ White Sauce
1934

1 tbsp. butter
1 tbsp. flour
1 c. milk
½ tsp. salt

Melt butter in a skillet; add flour and salt, and stir to blend. Add milk and stir until thickened. This makes a thin white sauce, useful for cream soups and as a sauce for vegetables.

❦ Pea Soufflé
October 1916

1 c. fresh peas
1 tsp. salt
pepper to taste
4 tbsp. milk
4 egg whites

Wash peas and put them on to boil; boil till tender. Press through sieve, then add salt, pepper, and milk. Beat egg whites till stiff and fold into pea mixture. Butter a baking dish and bake at 350°F for 20–30 minutes. Soufflés should be served as soon as removed from the oven.

❦ Pea and Carrot Casserole
January 1932

6 slices bacon, cut in small pieces
2 c. White Sauce (pg. 89)
1½ c. cooked peas
1½ c. sliced cooked carrots
4 c. mashed potatoes

Brown the bacon in a skillet, reserve fat. Prepare the white sauce. In a greased casserole, arrange in alternate layers the peas and carrots. Add the bacon and 2 tbsp. of bacon fat to the white sauce and pour it over the vegetables. Cover top with potatoes and bake for 20 minutes at 400°F.

❧ String Beans

May 1936

The secret of really good string beans, whether you serve them hot or cold, lies in their preparation. Do be sure to slice them in long, very thin slivers instead of breaking them crosswise. The beans look and taste so much better, and there is a new cutter on the market for just this purpose. When the day comes to stretch the beans, think of bean salad. This is a German recipe, popular with men as well as women.

—The Farmer's Wife Magazine

Add to cooled, cooked green beans just half their quantity of thinly sliced cucumbers. Marinate both with French Salad Dressing (pg. 181) in which a small onion has been grated. Serve on lettuce or in a bowl, and then, oh the taste!

❧ String Beans with Bacon

July 1911

1 qt. well-ripened
   string beans
1 pt. boiling water
¼ lb. bacon, diced

Remove the strings from beans, cut in ⅛-inch lengths, add the boiling water and bacon, and cook very tender, adding more water if necessary. Salt and pepper to taste.

Dessert

No self-respecting farm wife would have dreamed of serving dinner or supper without dessert of some sort. At harvest time these were usually simple affairs, since so many of them were required to feed large crews. Although, pie and the occasional ice cream was known to be served with enthusiastic results.

TABLE TALK
August 1914
Sarah A. Cooke

With the fried chicken we served a chocolate pudding, or any simple boiled pudding which takes but a few minutes' preparation on top of the stove. It is served with sweetened cream flavored with vanilla or lemon. With the boiled meat we served a peach or berry cobbler, using canned fruit to save time. Sometimes we varied this with an applesauce pudding. A huge pan of this pudding may be prepared in the time it takes to make one pie.

If one avoids the vegetables which require much time for picking and preparation, the desserts which require so much fussing either for preparation or serving, and have plenty of the simple things well cooked, the men will be just as well satisfied. Hard-working men always relish good, plain food.

❧ Steamed Chocolate Pudding with Sterling Sauce
February 1938

½ c. unsalted butter
1 c. sugar
1 egg, beaten
2 c. cake flour
¼ tsp. salt
1 tbsp. baking powder
1 c. milk
3 oz. bittersweet
   chocolate
1 tsp. vanilla

Cream butter, add sugar gradually, and then egg. Sift flour, salt, and baking powder, then add alternately with milk. Melt chocolate over low flame in a double boiler, then add with vanilla. Turn into twelve to fourteen small buttered molds, custard cups, or ramekins, filling two-thirds full. Cover with waxed paper and steam over gently boiling water for 1½ hours, adding more water to the steamer as necessary. Serve hot with:

Sterling Sauce:
¾ c. butter
2 c. light brown sugar
½ c. heavy cream
2 tsp. vanilla

Cream butter and sugar very thoroughly. Add cream gradually to prevent separation. The mixture will be fluffy and smooth. Put in double boiler and when sugar is dissolved, add vanilla. Serve hot or cold.

❦ Cherry Batter Pudding

June 1927

1–1 ½ lbs. cherries, stoned
sugar
1 c. flour
2 tsp. baking powder
½ c. milk
1 tsp. unsalted butter, melted

Fill baking dish three-quarters full of stoned cherries tossed with sugar. Sift dry ingredients, add milk and butter, beat till smooth, and spread over the fruit. Bake till brown at 350°F. Serve with Fruit Sauce:

Fruit Sauce:
2 c. fruit juice
1 tbsp. cornstarch
3 tbsp. flour
sugar, if needed
pinch salt
1 tsp. unsalted butter

Heat the juice. Mix cornstarch, flour, sugar, and salt and blend into juice. Cook 10 minutes over medium-low flame, stirring while it thickens. Remove from fire and add butter. Beat thoroughly and serve.

❦ Apple Batter Pudding
October 1912

Pare, core, and quarter eight apples. Place in a baking dish with 1 c. sugar and a sprinkling of cinnamon. Bake at 350°F for about ½ hour, until half done. Then pour over them the following batter:

2 pts. flour, 1 tsp. salt, 1 tsp. baking powder; mix then rub in 1 c. butter. Beat two eggs and add to 2 c. milk. Stir this into the dry mixture.

After batter has been poured over apples, finish baking. Serve with lemon sauce:

Lemon Sauce:
Make a syrup of 1½ c. sugar and 1 c. water. Boil 10 minutes. Add 4 tbsp. butter and 4 tbsp. lemon juice.

❦ Bread Pudding
June 1925

2 c. stale breadcrumbs
1 qt. scalded milk
1 c. sugar
2 eggs, well beaten
½ tsp. salt
2 tbsp. butter
1 tsp. vanilla OR ¼ tsp. cinnamon and nutmeg OR grated orange or
   lemon rind

Soak bread in milk, cool, and add remaining ingredients. Bake at 350°F for 1 hour. Serve with any desired sauce. A much finer pudding may be made by using four eggs. Put two eggs and two yolks in the pudding. Make a meringue of the remaining whites, stiffly beaten with 2 tbsp. sugar added and beaten again. Spread this over warm pudding and return to oven till well puffed and delicately browned. This is good either hot or cold.

❦ Corn Pudding
October 1915

Scrape pulp from twelve large ears of sweet corn. Add five beaten eggs, 1 qt. milk, 1 tbsp. sugar, 2 tbsp. butter, and 1 tsp. salt. Place in a buttered, covered dish and bake 1 hour at 350°F. Remove cover and cook several minutes longer, till browned. Serve hot.

❦ Banana Pudding
December 1929
Contributed by Mrs. J.M.B., South Carolina

1 c. milk
1 c. sugar
2 eggs, well beaten
1 tsp. vanilla
3 large bananas
vanilla wafers
½ lb. marshmallows

Make a soft custard by cooking gently (do not boil!) until thick: milk, sugar, eggs, and vanilla. Stir constantly. Slice bananas, arranging them alternately with wafers in a casserole or baking dish. Pour custard over this and place marshmallows, cut in halves, over top. Put in oven a few minutes to brown.

❧ Steamed Cocoa Pudding

October 1917

1 tbsp. butter
½ c. sugar
1 egg, beaten
½ c. milk
1¼ c. flour
3 tsp. baking powder
6 tbsp. cocoa powder
¼ c. boiling water

Cream the butter and sugar; add the egg, the milk, and then the flour and baking powder mixed together. Make a smooth paste of the cocoa and boiling water and add to the flour mixture. Steam 1 hour in a well-greased, covered mold, or ½ hour if individual molds are used.

❧ Peach Pudding

September 1912

Butter a pudding dish and place whole peaches on the bottom of it—six to eight peaches in all. Pour over them a batter made of 1 c. milk, 1 c. sugar, one egg, 2 tbsp. butter, 2 tsp. baking powder, and enough flour to make a drop batter—2–3 c. Drop this over the peaches and bake at 375°F until nicely browned. Serve with cream.

❦ Pennsylvania Rice Pudding
July–August 1921

2 qts. whole milk
½ c. sugar
1½ tsp. salt
⅔ c. raisins
½ c. uncooked rice, rinsed
nutmeg, if liked

Put milk, sugar, salt, raisins, and washed rice into a large baking dish. Place in an oven at 350°F and bake 2½–3 hours. Stir very often for the first hour. The pudding should be of a creamy consistency. May be served hot or cold. This amount will serve 8 or 10.

❦ Tapioca Cream
1934

3 tbsp. quick-cooking tapioca
¼ tsp. salt
3 c. scalded milk
⅓ c. sugar
1 tsp. vanilla
2 egg yolks, beaten
2 egg whites, beaten stiff
sliced fresh fruit, as in peaches or bananas

Add tapioca and salt to hot milk and cook in double boiler according to package directions on tapioca. Stir frequently. Add sugar and vanilla to yolks and stir in 2 tbsp. tapioca mixture, then return all to double boiler and cook 3 minutes. Cool and fold in egg whites. When thoroughly chilled, pour cream over fruit and serve.

❦ Fruit Cobbler
1934

1 c. flour
⅓ c sugar
¼ tsp. salt
1 tsp. baking powder
¼ c. milk
1 egg, beaten
1 tsp. melted butter
1½ c. fresh stoned cherries, chopped apples, cleaned berries, etc.

Sift dry ingredients together and add milk, egg, and butter. Mix and pour over fruit arranged on bottom of buttered baking dish. Bake 25 minutes at 400°F till brown. Serve hot.

❦ Rhubarb Crisp
April 1935

2 c. diced rhubarb
1 tsp. cinnamon
⅛ c. sugar
¼ c. water
1 c. oatmeal
½ c. butter
1 c. brown sugar

In bottom of buttered baking dish place fruit, cinnamon, sugar, and water. Mix oatmeal, butter, and sugar and pat over top. Bake at 350°F for 40 minutes. Serve with cream.

❦ Plain Pastry—2 Crusts
1934

(Double this recipe to make two pies)

½ tsp. salt
1½ c. sifted flour
½ c. lard
3 or 4 tbsp. ice cold water

Add salt to flour and cut in shortening with a dough blender, sharp-tined fork, or fingertips, until pieces are size of small peas. Add a little water at a time, mixing with a fork lightly until it can be shaped into a ball. Divide dough and roll out one crust at a time.

■ ■

❦ Buttermilk Pie
September 1934
Contributed by Mrs. S.G.P., Wisconsin

2 tbsp. butter
2 tbsp. flour
2 egg yolks and 1 whole egg
1½ c. sugar
1 tbsp. lemon juice
2½ c. buttermilk
Meringue (pg. 140)

Cream the butter and flour together. Add the beaten yolks and whole egg. Add sugar, lemon juice, and buttermilk, stirring well. Pour into pie plates lined with rich pastry and bake at 450°F for 10 minutes before lowering to 350°F. Use two leftover egg whites for Meringue (pg. 140).

❦ Apple Pie
September 1913

Peel, slice, and chop (not fine) 2 qts. tart apples. Line two deep pie pans with pastry, then add to each dish of apples ½ c. butter, ½ c. sugar, and a sprinkle of ground cinnamon. Cover with top crusts and bake at 350°F until apples are tender. Serve warm.

❦ Pies for a Week
1934

Two quarts of flour will be ample for twelve 8-inch, single-crust pies. On that basis the recipe is as follows:

3½ c. shortening
2 level tbsp. salt
2 qts. flour
cold water to make dough

Work the fat into the salt and flour lightly with the tips of the fingers. (Too vigorous mixing toughens the crust, and if the lard is too finely divided the crust will be less flaky.) The amount of water cannot be definitely stated because different flours differ in hardness, and very cold ingredients require more water than warm. Pour the water a little at a time into small wells made in the mixed flour and fat. Lift the dry ingredients through the water on the tips of the fingers, being careful not to knead the dough. When the dough is sufficiently moist it will clean the sides of the mixing bowl. Stop at this point and handle each pie from then on separately. Materials and utensils should at all times be kept as cold as possible.

❧ Cottage Cheese Pie
October 1933

⅔ c. milk

½ c. sugar combined with 2 tbsp. flour

1 egg yolk, beaten

1 c. cottage cheese

2 tbsp. butter

juice and grated rind of 1 lemon

Meringue (pg. 140)

Heat milk, add slowly to sugar and flour, then return to top portion of double boiler. Cook mixture till thick, stirring constantly. Add egg yolk and cook till egg thickens. Add cheese, butter, and lemon. Pour into a well-baked crust. Cover with Meringue (pg. 140) and brown at 300°F.

❧ Banana Cream Pie
1934

2 c. rich milk

½ c. sugar

¼ c. cornstarch or ⅓ c. flour

¼ tsp. salt

2 egg yolks, beaten

1 tsp. vanilla

2 bananas, sliced

Meringue (pg. 140)

Scald 1¾ milk in top of double boiler. Mix remaining ¼ c. milk with sugar, cornstarch, and salt and add to milk. Cook 10 minutes, stirring constantly. Add egg yolks to mixture, stirring a little of the hot custard into eggs first. Cook 3–5 minutes; add vanilla and cool slightly. Pour in baked shell over several layers of sliced banana. Cover with Meringue (pg. 140) and bake 20 minutes.

Variation:

Strawberry or Pineapple Cream Pie: Fresh sliced strawberries or canned pineapple may be used in place of bananas.

❦ Cocoanut Cream Pie

October 1931

Contributed by Mrs. Nora Townner

unbaked pie pastry
2 c. milk or cocoanut milk
2 eggs, separated
¼ tsp. salt

3 tbsp. sugar
1 c. grated unsweetened cocoanut
Meringue (pg. 140)

Line a pie tin with uncooked pie pastry, then add filling mixture made with milk, egg yolks, salt, sugar, and cocoanut as in regular custards. Bake at 450°F for 10 minutes, then reduce heat to 350°F and continue cooking for 30 minutes. Make Meringue with leftover egg whites (pg. 140). Spread on top of pie and bake until golden brown.

❦ Cherry Cream Pie

June 1910

Line a plate with nice pastry, add 2 c. stoned cherries and 1 c. sugar, and bake at 400°F until nearly done; then, pour over it one egg, beaten lightly and mixed with ½ c. rich sweet cream. Return to oven at 375°F and finish baking until the custard is set.

❦ Fruit Pie
1934

¼ to ⅓ c. flour
1 to 1½ c. sugar
¼ tsp. salt
1 qt. fruit, washed and prepared
2 tbsp. butter

Thoroughly mix flour, sugar, and salt. (Use smaller amounts of sugar and flour with sweet fruits.) Mix this with fruit and turn into pie tin lined with unbaked pastry. Dot with butter. Put ½-inch strips of pastry, lattice fashion, over the top. Bake 15 minutes at 450°F and then at 350°F for remainder of baking.

Fruits such as blueberries, gooseberries, peaches, rhubarb, and cherries may be used. Two good combinations: equal parts currants and huckleberries or five sliced, tart apples with a few huckleberries tossed in.

❦ Lemon "Cake" Pie
July 1931

1 c. sugar
3 tbsp. flour
¼ c. butter, softened
3 eggs, separated
juice and grated rind of 1 lemon
2 c. milk

Mix sugar and flour and slightly softened butter. Add slightly beaten egg yolks, then lemon, and when well blended add milk. Fold in beaten egg whites and bake in pie crust at 325°F about 40 minutes. Makes two small (8-inch) pies with custard in bottom and sponge cake on top.

FARM WOMEN'S LETTERS
May 1936

Dear Editor: A friend from the city spent the holidays with us, and upon leaving remarked how wonderful it was to have a few days' vacation in the country, but how very monotonous to live there—no amusements, no broadening influences, no access to art or literature. Humph! She need not patronize me!

Summer—alfalfa curing; the first rooster big enough for the frying pan; jelly glasses cooling in the north window; warm afternoons when the cattle drowse in the willow shade; the men grateful for cold buttermilk and ginger cookies after a turn in the grain field; the young folks coming home from a dip in the creek, their voices sweet in the moonlight.

Letters *from*

Farm Women

❦ Angel Food Cake
April 1937

1 c. sifted cake flour
1 ⅓ c. sugar
1 ½ c. egg whites
½ tsp. salt
1 tsp. cream of tartar
2 tbsp. water
1 tsp. vanilla

Sift flour once before measuring, then sift again with ⅓ c. of the sugar. Beat egg whites with a rotary beater, adding salt, cream of tartar, water, and vanilla when they are foamy. Beat whites just until they peak and are still moist and shiny. With flat beater or mixing spoon, fold in remaining sugar, sifting 1 or 2 tbsp. at a time over surface and gently folding it in (about fifty strokes). Fold sifted flour and sugar mixture in the same way (about ninety strokes). Pour into ungreased angel food cake pans, and bake immediately in slow oven (325°F) for 1 hour or until surface of cake, when pressed lightly with finger, springs back into place. It should be at its full height, have a delicate brown color, and be shrunken slightly from the pan. Let cool in the inverted pan 1 hour before removing.

❦ Crisp Crumb Torte

April 1935
Contributed by Miss A.C.G., Nebraska

3 egg whites
1 c. sugar
½ tsp. almond extract
½ tsp. vanilla
½ c. chopped dates
½ c. chopped nuts
½ c. bran crumbs

Beat whites, adding sugar gradually, then flavoring, fruit, and nuts. Fold in crumbs. Pour into buttered baking pan and bake at 300°F till dry on top and pale brown—40–50 minutes. To serve, cut in squares and serve with whipped cream. This may be baked in two small pie tins and layers put together with a cream filling.

❦ Sour Milk Gingerbread

September 1934

2¾ c. flour
½ c. sugar
1½ tsp. baking powder
1 tsp. baking soda
½ tsp. salt
1 tsp. ground ginger
½ tsp. ground cloves
½ tsp. cinnamon
1 egg
1 c. buttermilk
1 c. molasses
¼ c. fat, melted

Sift dry ingredients. Beat egg thoroughly, then add buttermilk, molasses, and melted fat. Combine liquid and dry ingredients thoroughly. Pour into well-greased shallow pan. Bake 60 minutes at 325°F.

Pineapple Upside-Down Cake

September 1938

Upside-down cakes are easy to make and require but little time for preparation. The following recipe is one that has been successfully tried by women of rural Kentucky with different toppings.

—The Farmer's Wife Magazine

Cake:

1½ c. flour

1 c. sugar

2 tsp. baking powder

½ tsp. salt

2 eggs, broken into a 1-cup measuring cup, which is then filled with rich milk or cream

1 tsp. vanilla

Sift dry ingredients together, add liquids, and beat hard for five minutes.

Topping:

1 small can pineapple, crushed or sliced, ¾ c. juice reserved

¾ c. brown sugar

4 tbsp. butter

unsweetened whipped cream

Place pineapple juice, brown sugar, and butter in a 9-inch cast-iron skillet. Bring to a boil and boil for 2 minutes. Place pineapple in the juice and cover with the batter, spreading it so it covers all the fruit. Bake at 375°F for 30 minutes. Let stand until partly cool, then turn upside down on cake plate or platter to serve. Accompany with unsweetened whipped cream.

It is essential to beat the batter until it is smooth and fluffy for a light cake of fine texture. In blending the brown sugar, butter, and fruit juice, do not boil the syrup until it becomes thick and candy-like. Let it boil only long enough to blend together well.

Sour Cream Cake with Variations

May 1935
Contributed by Mrs. H.M.S., Washington

1 c. sour cream
1 c. sugar
2 eggs, separated
1 tsp. vanilla
2 c. cake flour or 1¾ c. all-purpose flour
2 tsp. baking powder
1 tsp. baking soda
½ tsp. salt

Place cream, sugar, vanilla, and egg yolks in a mixing bowl and beat till light and fluffy. Add dry ingredients, then fold in stiffly beaten egg whites. Bake in a flat rectangular pan (8x10-inch or 9x9-inch) for 35 minutes at 325°F.

Banana Cream Cake: Add 3 bananas, mashed, to cream, egg, and sugar mixture and continue as above. Serve warm, cut in squares and topped with whipped cream.

Spice Cake: Sift with dry ingredients: 1 tsp. each cinnamon and nutmeg and ½ tsp. ground cloves. Add ½ c. chopped dates and grated rind of half an orange before combining with cream mixture.

❦ Devil's Food Cake
1934

2 oz. bittersweet chocolate
2 tbsp. brown sugar
1 c. milk
1 tsp. salt
⅓ c. butter
1 c. white sugar
2 eggs
1 ½ c. flour
1 tsp. baking soda
1 tsp. vanilla

Melt chocolate in a double boiler. Add brown sugar, milk, and salt. Stir till smooth, then remove from heat and cool. Cream butter and add sugar, beating till creamy. Add eggs and mix. Sift in dry ingredients alternately with chocolate. Add vanilla and mix well. Pour batter into two buttered cake pans. Bake 30 minutes at 350°F. Put layers together and frost with Seven-Minute Icing (see below).

Seven-Minute Icing:
2 c. sugar
2 egg whites
½ c. water
2 tbsp. honey
few grains salt
1 tsp. vanilla

Put all ingredients except vanilla in the top of a double boiler. Cook over boiling water 7–10 minutes, beating all the while with a rotary beater. When ready to remove from the stove, the icing will be thick and almost ready to spread. Add vanilla, beating until cool and ready to spread.

❧ Banana Cake
1934

½ c. butter
1½ c. sugar
2 egg yolks
1 tsp. baking soda
4 tbsp. sour cream
2 c. cake flour, sifted
½ c. water
1 c. mashed bananas
1 tsp. vanilla

Cream butter while adding sugar gradually, then add yolks. Mix baking soda in sour cream and add alternately with half the sifted flour. Add water alternately with remaining flour. Add bananas and vanilla and pour batter into flat, buttered baking dish. Bake at 375°F for 45 minutes to 1 hour.

❧ Basic Honey Cake
August 1933

½ c. butter
½ c. honey
½ c. sugar
2 eggs, beaten
2 c. cake flour
2 tsp. baking soda
4 tsp. baking powder
¼ tsp. salt
⅓ c. milk
2 tsp. cream

Cream butter, honey, and sugar. Add beaten eggs and beat till blended. Sift dry ingredients and add alternately with milk. Do not beat, just mix slightly to blend. Add cream and pour batter into two buttered-papered-buttered 8-inch cake pans. Bake at 350°F for 20 minutes.

❧ Baked Bananas
May 1931

Use four ripe bananas, skin and scrape off any stringy fibers. Split the bananas lengthwise and place in one layer in buttered baking dish. Sprinkle with 2 tbsp. sugar and the juice of one lemon. Dot with bits of unsalted butter. Add ⅓ c. cold water and bake at 350°F till bananas are delicately brown, about 20 minutes. Baste occasionally. Serve with whipped cream.

"Whhat shall we have for dessert?" This question, especially in hot weather, faces the house mother seven times a week. Frozen desserts are a sensing and saving answer to the "vexed" question.

A simple ice cream takes no more time to make than a cake or pie. One freezing can be made to serve for more than one meal. And for a "company" dessert, what better aid can you summon?

—The Farmer's Wife Magazine, *July 1917*

❧ French Vanilla Ice Cream
1934

2 c. milk
4 egg yolks
⅔ c. sugar
⅛ tsp. salt
2 c. cream
½ tsp. vanilla

Scald milk in double boiler and
pour slowly, whisking all the while,
over egg yolks mixed with sugar and
salt. Return to double boiler and simmer till
the mixture coats a spoon. Chill in refrigerator,
add cream and vanilla, and freeze in an ice cream
maker according to manufacturer's instructions.

Variations:
Peanut Brittle Ice Cream: Grind peanut brittle to make 1 c. and add when ice
cream is partially frozen.

Peppermint Ice Cream: Grind peppermint candy to equal 1 c. Omit vanilla
and decrease sugar to ½ c. in foundation recipe. Add candy when ice
cream is partially frozen.

Sour Cream Chocolate Ice Cream: To the foundation custard recipe add 2 oz.
melted bittersweet chocolate and chill. Replace cream with 1 c. milk and
1 c. sour cream mixed with ⅓ c. sugar.

❧ Strawberry Ice Cream
July 1917

4 c. strawberries
1 c. sugar
6 egg yolks
1 qt. half and half
pinch salt

Wash berries thoroly, hull, and cover with half the sugar. Mash together and set aside. Mix yolks, half and half, salt, and remaining sugar, and heat over medium flame till bubbles just begin to form at the edges, but do not allow to boil. Allow to cool, then mix with strawberry mixture. Place in ice cream maker and freeze according to manufacturer's directions.

❧ Maple Parfait
July 1923

4 eggs
1 c. hot maple syrup
1 pt. heavy cream

Beat eggs slightly and slowly pour over maple syrup. Cook till mixture thickens, cool, and add cream beaten till stiff. Place in ice cream maker and freeze according to manufacturer's directions.

❧ Chocolate Sauce for Ice Cream
July 1933

1 c. sugar
½ c. cocoa powder
1 tbsp. flour

1 c. boiling water
1 tbsp. butter

Combine dry ingredients and add hot water, stirring continually. Cook till desired thickness is reached. Add butter and cool.

Everyday Meals from Harvest-Time Bounty

"Make hay while the sun shines" is the motto to follow now, and your vegetable garden is the place where it can be applied most effectively. Why neglect your garden and pay outrageous prices next winter for the stuff out of somebody else's garden put up in tin cans?

—The Farmer's Wife Magazine

July brings harvest days to the farm and usually extra men to feed, but to make the problem somewhat easier, July also finds the garden and berry patches at their best. The housewife who uses vegetables and fruits in abundance makes her meals that much more interesting and provides her family with the very best kind of diet.

—The Farmer's Wife Magazine

❧ Baked Stuffed Green Peppers
June 1922

12 sweet green peppers
2 c. breadcrumbs
2 c. chopped leftover meat
2 eggs, slightly beaten
2 tbsp. melted butter
milk to moisten
salt and pepper

Select large, smooth peppers, cut a round opening in stem ends, remove seeds and pulp, and soak in cold water for half an hour. Fill with mixture of breadcrumbs; leftover meat; slightly beaten eggs; butter; enough milk to form a soft, moist mixture; and seasoning. Place in a baking dish and bake at 375°F for 40 minutes, or till peppers are tender. Serve from baking dish or platter.

Turnips Delicious
July–August 1921

Pare, slice, and cube turnips into small cubes. Put to cook in boiling water to just cover. When tender and water has boiled down some, add butter, pepper, and salt and allow the water to all boil out. Stir thoroughly after the butter is added so that all are thoroughly seasoned.

Dutch Lettuce Slaw
May 1927

3 large heads lettuce
1 qt. mashed potatoes, hot
butter
salt and pepper

sour cream
4 slices bacon
6 scallions
1 c. vinegar

Wash lettuce in water, rinse and shake dry, and shred very fine. Season potatoes well with butter, salt and pepper, and sour cream. Beat till fluffy. Fry sliced bacon till almost done and drain. Cut scallions, tops and all, and cook in bacon fat till softened, then add vinegar. Combine all together.

Squash is one of the oldest and most typically American vegetables, known to be here when white men came exploring. When once we become well acquainted with the squash family, we seldom lack variety in our vegetable dishes. There is the whole range: from zucchini, which cooks in less than 10 minutes, to handsome, orange-brown squares of baked hubbard squash, which require 1 or more hours. Summer varieties are so tender and thin-skinned when they first come on that we slice them through to cook and serve, skin, seeds, and all.

—The Farmer's Wife Magazine

❧ Italian Squash (Zucchini)
October 1935

Slice or cut lengthwise in strips and cook in a small amount of boiling salted water until barely tender; drain and serve with melted butter or cream. They are especially delicious sautéed or fried in cooking oil or butter along with a few very thin slices of onion, then sprinkled with salt and paprika.

❧ Baked Acorn Squash
July–August 1921

Cut squash in half, place with cut side down on pie tin in the oven, and bake at 350°F till done, about 45 minutes–1 hour. Remove from shell, mash, and season with salt, pepper, and butter.

❦ Baked Summer Squash and Corn
October 1935

Cut tender summer squash in thick slices, then lay in bottom of greased
baking dish. Brush with butter and sprinkle with salt. Add a thick layer of
uncooked corn kernels and sprinkle with salt and pepper. Cover dish closely
and bake at 350°F for 20 to 30 minutes. Remove lid, cover with slices of
peeled tomato, and sprinkle lightly with salt and sugar. Top with thin slices of
bacon, return to oven, and bake at 400°F or broil till bacon is crisp.

❦ Stuffed Summer Squash
October 1935

Cut large summer squashes in halves. Remove seeds. Steam or bake at
350°F till nearly tender and put in a baking dish. A good stuffing is made
as follows:

2 slices onion, diced fine
2 tbsp. celery, diced
3 tbsp. melted butter
1 c. soft breadcrumbs
1 c. chopped browned beef
salt and pepper

Cook onion and celery in butter till soft, then add crumbs and meat and
heat through. Add a little melted butter if meat is quite lean. Stuff squash,
top with thin slices of peeled tomato, and top with very thin strips of bacon
or bits of butter. Bake at 350°F till heated through and brown on top.
Two other good fillings are crumbs and crumbled crisp bacon, and mixed
and seasoned vegetables such as corn, green beans, or tomatoes.

 Watercress
July 1920

A Cress Bed for Every Farm

Watercress is one of the most delicious salad vegetables and one which can be on nearly every farm. It requires no weeding and very little care and will furnish a most excellent food from earliest spring until the pond or creek freezes. If you have a spring or creek on the farm where cress is already growing, you are fortunate. If not, you will never regret any trouble spent to set out a bed. The bank of a shallow stream whose current is not too swift makes a good location for cress. It grows as close to the water as it can, and even in the water.

In gathering cress, use scissors. This will enable one not to disturb the long, glistening rootlets and will ensure a permanent supply. Wash the leaves carefully so that they will be free from sand. The stems are as delicious as the leaves.

Watercress may be used in every way that lettuce is used, with Mayonnaise or French Salad Dressing (pg. 181) or with only a sprinkling of salt. It makes plain bread and butter a real feast. Serve with fruit salads or with any kind of vegetable salad. Use as a filling for sandwiches. Serve with fish, game, or chicken.

STRAWBERRIES REMIND ME
June 1912
Lulu G. Parker

"What cause set free so much of red from heats at cure of earth, and mixed such sweets with sour and spice?" Perfect strawberries served whole with sugar and cream are fit for kings without further trimming. But sometimes one has not enough to serve the potluck guest, or they are not all good enough to serve whole. Then these "fussier" ways give variety and make the fruit go farther inexpensively.

❦ Strawberry Pudding
June 1912

Beat 1 tsp. butter to a cream, add gradually 1½ c. powdered sugar and the beaten white of an egg. Beat until very light, add 1 pt. mashed strawberries, and serve immediately with two or three whole berries on each plate.

Strawberry Float
June 1912

Make a boiled custard with the yolks of two eggs (more if you can afford it), 1 qt. milk, ½ c. sugar, and ½ tsp. vanilla. Crush and strain 1 pt. strawberries and mix into them ½ c. powdered sugar. Beat the whites of the eggs into the fruit. Serve the custard in the bottom of glass cups with the strawberry float on top.

Use the juice which was strained off the strawberries diluted with water for a refreshing drink.

If berries are sandy or dirty so that they require washing, do this before the hulls are removed by putting them into a colander and gently pouring water over; or a still better way is to dip them one at a time, when hulling, into a bowl of cold water.

Strawberry Trifle
June 1913
I hope no one will omit the Strawberry Trifle.

—The Farmer's Wife Magazine

Line a glass dish with alternate layers of macaroons and sugared strawberries. Make a custard of the yolks of three eggs, ¼ c. sugar, and 1½ c. milk—heat the milk till almost bubbling over a medium-low heat; add a few tablespoons to the eggs and sugar, which have been beaten together, then add the egg mixture to the milk on the stove, stirring briskly until the custard is thick and smooth. Cool and pour over the contents of the dish. Whip the whites of the eggs till very stiff, put into a buttered pudding dish, cover, and cook in a double boiler for 20 minutes. Allow to cool before placing over the custard and sprinkling with crushed macaroons. Serve very cold and this is delicious.

Old-Fashioned Strawberry Shortcake
1934

2 heaping c. flour
2 tsp. baking powder
¼ tsp. salt
2 tsp. sugar
¼ c. butter
¾ c. milk
plenty of strawberries

Mix the dry ingredients and sift. Rub in the butter with the tips of the fingers and add milk gradually. Toss on a floured board, divide into two parts, pat and roll out, and bake in buttered and floured layer cake tins at 400°F for 15 minutes. Split and butter. Sweeten strawberries to taste and place on the back of the stove till warmed. Crush slightly and put between and on top of the shortcake. Cover the top with whipped cream, sweetened and flavored with vanilla extract—to 1 c. cream add ¼ c. sugar and ½ tsp. vanilla.

Pineapples and Strawberries with Mint
June 1936

Ingredients required are sliced pineapple, or fresh pineapple cut in wedges; fresh strawberries, halved; fresh mint; and powdered sugar. Arrange each serving on a few springs of mint. First place pineapple slices or wedges, then berries. Top with a spoonful of mint, chopped and mixed with powdered sugar. An unusually refreshing combination.

❦ Blackberry Gingerbread Upside-Down Cake
September 1938

2 c. flour
½ c. sugar
1 tsp. ground ginger
1 tsp. cinnamon
½ tsp. allspice
¼ tsp. salt

½ tsp. baking soda
1½ tsp. baking powder
1 egg
¾ c. molasses
½ c. melted butter
¾ c. hot water

Sift dry ingredients together; then mix together egg, molasses, butter, and hot water; add dry ingredients. Beat till well blended. For the topping:

4 tbsp. butter
¾ c. berry juice
¾ c. brown sugar
2 c. blackberries, washed and drained

In a 9-inch cast-iron skillet, bring butter, juice, and sugar to a boil and boil 2 minutes. Add berries, then pour in batter carefully to cover all fruit. Bake at 350°F for 35 minutes. Let stand in pan 15 minutes before turning out, inverted, onto a plate or cake stand.

❦ Blackberry Roly-poly
August 1938

2 c. flour
½ tsp. salt
1 tbsp. baking powder
¼ c. butter

¾ c. milk
2 c. blackberries
⅔ c. sugar

Sift dry ingredients together, cut in butter, stir in milk, turn out on board, and knead lightly. Roll out ¼ inch thick, spread berries over dough, and sprinkle with sugar, leaving a margin of dough all around. Roll up as for jelly roll, sealing edges. Tie roll loosely in a cloth, place on pie pan, and steam 1 hour. Serve warm, cut in thick slices, and pass a pitcher of cream, sweetened and flavored with nutmeg.

❦ Frosted Berries

June 1936
Contributed by Mrs. G.A.C, Louisiana

2 tbsp. butter, softened
½ c. powdered sugar
1 tbsp. cream
fine berries, unhulled

Cream butter, add sugar, and blend thoroughly. Add cream to moisten. Dip tips of berries (washed and dried) in this icing and chill thoroughly. Serve on strawberry-leaf-garnished plate.

❦ Blackberry Pudding

August 1913

A very good dessert for when blackberries make their appearance is an old-fashioned blackberry pudding, which is not difficult to make and is usually very much liked by the children. Have already in separate dishes 3 c. blackberries and 1 qt. flour sifted with 2 tbsp. baking powder. Beat separately the yolks and whites of three eggs. Add to the yolks 2 c. milk and then stir in the whites carefully. To this mixture add the flour a little at a time, then stir in the blackberries, which should be dredged with a little flour just as they are added to the batter. Turn the pudding into a deep, greased dish and bake 1 hour at 375°F. During the first three-quarters of an hour put a cover over the top, so that the lower part of the pudding will not get thoroughly baked, before removing the cover to brown the top. Serve hot with Hard Sauce. The secret of success with this pudding is in having the eggs very light and in quickly mixing all the ingredients. If this is done, the pudding will be digestible and palatable and free from that "sogginess" so characteristic of poorly made fruit puddings.

Hard Sauce:

Mix together ½ c. sweet butter, ½ c. heavy cream, and 1 c. sugar and boil gently for 5–6 minutes over a medium-high flame. Add ½ tsp. vanilla or lemon extract and stir to mix. Remove from heat and serve.

Raspberries served with sugar and cream are one of the treats of summertime. But if the season is generous in supplying the right proportion of rain and sunshine, the family having its own berry patch will be glad to see the fruit appearing in cool drinks, fresh salads, and tempting desserts before the last of the berries are gone.

—The Farmer's Wife Magazine

❦ Raspberry Cream
June 1929

For this dessert, fresh graham crackers are crumbled finely and mixed with crushed berries, placed in a tall, slender glass, and covered with more than their bulk of stiffly beaten cream, sweetened to taste and dotted with whole hickory nutmeats.

❦ Raspberry Pudding Sauce
June 1929

Bring 1 c. raspberry juice and ½ tsp. lemon juice to the boiling point. Make a smooth paste of ½ tbsp. cornstarch and a little cold water and add it to the boiling mixture, stirring constantly while it cooks. Add sugar to taste and boil a moment longer. Serve hot over ice cream.

Gooseberries are the backward children of the berry family. Like the modest, retiring members of the human clan, their virtues and latent possibilities are often overlooked. So it seems only fair and just that someone should champion the cause of this down-trodden member of the berry family. So here and now we make a plea for the plain, retiring and almost-forgotten Mr. Goose Berry. Our grandmothers, who knew him more intimately, were very fond of him. They knew how to get the most out of him, and found him very adaptable.

—The Farmer's Wife Magazine

Gooseberry Trifle
July 1928

Stem, wash, and put into a saucepan 1 qt. gooseberries with sufficient granulated sugar to sweeten them—about 1 c. Boil until soft. Put into the bottom of a serving dish and cover with a custard made by heating 1 pt. milk and adding to it ½ c. sugar, 1 tbsp. cornstarch mixed smooth with a little cold milk, and two well-beaten eggs. Let custard boil till it thickens. When cold, cover with whipped cream.

Gooseberry Fool
July 1928

Rub through a sieve to remove the seeds 1 qt. stewed gooseberries. Add 1 c. sugar and 1 tbsp. melted butter before pulp has cooled. Whip in the yolks of three eggs which have been previously well beaten. When the mixture is light, put into a glass fruit dish and cover the top with whipped cream sweetened with 3 tbsp. powdered sugar.

August

Corn is king in the garden through the latter half of the summer growing season, and well it deserves to be. Whether served on the cob or cut off, whether served alone or cooked with other suitable foods, it is appetizing, satisfying, wholesome. The first corn of the season, coming to the table steaming hot, tender, and delicious, well buttered, is an event well worth waiting for most of a year. But other vegetables are abundant in the garden at this time of year, so make a big place for them also in your meal planning. Most of them provide food elements that every member of the family needs, especially growing children.

—The Farmer's Wife Magazine

MY SUMMER KITCHEN
August 1918
L.A. Crow

If there is anything on our farm that I could not do without it is our summer kitchen, the little two-room log house in which my husband and I started housekeeping. As the years passed and our family increased, we needed more room, so we moved it back to make room for a modern two-story house. It is now connected with the house by a broad, covered platform that is shaded and almost covered with a wild-grape vine. Both rooms have outside doors; the little old windows were made larger and several new ones added.

In the larger room is a large zinc-covered table and a smaller one fastened to the wall that can be lowered when not in use. Across one end is a cupboard reaching to the ceiling with a large drawer at the bottom; a smaller cupboard stands on the other side, then there is an old kitchen stove that burns either coal or wood, a new three-burner oil stove with a large oven, two straight back chairs, and a comfortable rocking chair.

Here the laundry is done all the year, and fruit and vegetable canning and most of the cooking during the summer. If I wish to boil a ham, roast, bake or cook anything that requires a long steady heat, I always go to the summer kitchen. It is an ideal place in the winter for making sausage at butchering time, and I can cook turnips, cabbage, and sauerkraut without any odor reaching the house to offend some fastidious member of my family.

In the smaller room is a cupboard, where I keep all the vegetable and flower seeds I gather for next year's planting. Here too are my garden tools and a well-equipped tool chest, with nails of all sizes. Many's the bit of repairing I do myself.

My summer kitchen is often turned into an emergency hospital for motherless chickens; more than one tiny pig here has been warmed, fed, and allowed to grunt and squeal itself back to life; and here, in a corner, is a piece of old buffalo robe where Tabby can raise her family and purr in safe comfort. There is always room in the summer kitchen for anything that is wanted near the house but not in the house.

Every spring the little building is whitewashed inside and out; it is such a clean, cheery, home-like place that no one ever passes its door without stopping; father lingers to chat with mother; the hired men look in as they go and come from the fields; and company always takes an enjoyable peep.

Stately hollyhocks grow in profusion near the doors, and one end of the roof is overrun with a sweet-scented honeysuckle; a clump of golden-glow peeps in at the window where the tomatoes on the sill ripen in the sun; great clusters of hop vine shade the south window, and here is a bed of parsley, mint, sage, thyme, chives, and dill, with a great mass of pink and white hardy phlox for pure joy.

The summer kitchen is my kingdom, where I reign supreme! I think a summer kitchen, on a farm, is as necessary for the work of a farm family as horses and plow are for cultivation of the farm.

❦ Boiled Corn

July 1938

After carefully removing husks and silk, plunge into rapidly boiling water. Boil 10 minutes. Remove and serve on a napkin or towel so spread on a platter that the corners may be drawn over to keep it hot. Do not overcook!

❦ Cream of Corn Soup

October 1910

To each quart of fresh corn, cut from the cob, add 3 pts. of water and boil until tender (about 5–10 minutes). Add 2 tbsp. of butter, which has been well-mixed with 1 tbsp. of flour. Season to taste with salt and pepper and allow it to boil up. Add 1 c. heavy cream just before serving.

❦ Cream of Corn Soup II

August 1913

Scald 4 qts. milk, add 4 pts. grated fresh corn, and cook for 10 minutes. Thicken with 2 tsp. cornstarch moistened with a little cold milk; for seasoning use 4 tsp. salt, a little white pepper, and ¼ c. butter. Add 4 c. heavy cream before serving.

❦ Fried Corn

August 1913

Put 1 tbsp. butter into a skillet and put over the fire to get hot enough to sputter. As soon as the butter browns a little, pour into the skillet 1 qt. fresh corn kernels. Sprinkle a few drops of water over the corn, season with salt and pepper, and cover tightly to prevent sticking; stir frequently. When cooked, add 1 c. milk. Let stay on stove long enough to get hot again and pour into a hot dish.

❦ Corn Souffle

August 1927

1 tbsp. butter
¼ c. flour
2 c. milk
1 c. chopped corn kernels
1 c. grated cheddar cheese
3 eggs, separated
½ tsp. salt

Melt the butter and add the flour and milk to make a sauce, stirring constantly. When thickened add the corn, cheese, yolks, and salt. Off the heat, fold in the whites, beaten stiffly. Turn into a buttered baking dish and bake at 350°F for 30 minutes.

❦ Corn Salad

July 1938

2 c. corn kernels, sautéed briefly in butter
2 c. diced cooked beets
1 tsp. minced onion
salad dressing

Mix all together and serve on crisp lettuce leaves.

❦ Fried Cucumbers

August 1929
Sound weird? In 1929 raw cucumbers were thought to be difficult to digest; they were almost always cooked before serving, or pickled.

3 large cucumbers
1 egg
fine breadcrumbs
butter
salt, pepper, paprika to taste

Pare the cucumbers and cut lengthwise, remove seeds, then cut in ¼-inch slices. Sprinkle generously with salt, pepper, and paprika. Beat the egg and mix with 2 tbsp. cold water. Dip in the cucumber slices, then dip in crumbs. Fry in butter till golden brown.

TOMATOES, RIPE AND GREEN

September 1913

Annie E. Harris

Considering the many uses to which it may be put, the tomato has, apart from its beauty, a good excuse for being. There is no end, apparently, to the variety of appetizing dishes which may be prepared from this vegetable fresh from the garden.

The fresh tomato is attractive and makes a cool and desirable hot weather dish served raw. They should be kept whole just before being sent to the table, because of their tendency to liquefy. So adaptable is the tomato that it can be used in any course of a dinner, or in any meal. It may be fried or baked for breakfast; stewed, stuffed, scalloped, jellied, or made into soup for dinner; it may be sliced raw and served at supper either with sugar or salad dressing.

❦ Fried Tomatoes

September 1913

Cut firm but ripe tomatoes in halves. For four tomatoes, heat 1 tbsp. butter in frying pan. Dip tomatoes in flour, put cut side down in pan, cover, and cook over a hot fire until browned. Transfer to a hot dish, sprinkle 1 tbsp. flour in the pan, stir, and add 1 c. milk; stir until thickened, season with salt and pepper, boil 1 minute, and pour around tomatoes.

❦ Stuffed Tomatoes with Cheese

October 1926

6 tomatoes	2 tbsp. butter
3 c. breadcrumbs	½ tsp. salt
1 tbsp. chopped onion	cheese

Remove the pulp from the tomatoes and mix with crumbs. Cook onion in butter 1 minute and mix with crumbs and seasoning. Stuff tomatoes and bake in a shallow buttered dish at 350°F for 10 minutes. Remove from oven and cover with slices of cheese. Return to oven till cheese is melted and serve at once.

❦ Fried Green Tomatoes

September 1928

Slice firm green tomatoes into half-inch slices. Sprinkle with a little salt and a generous amount of brown sugar. Dip the slices in dry bread or cracker crumbs, patting in as many crumbs as possible. Have ready in a frying pan melted drippings, or melted butter and lard. Brown the tomato slices well on one side, then turn and brown on the other. When browned and tender remove carefully to a serving platter and make a dressing out of the drippings by adding 1 cupful of milk and thickening it with 1 scant tbsp. of flour dissolved in a little cold water. Boil to cook the flour, salt to taste, and pour around the tomato slices.

❧ Tomatoes in Batter
August 1911

Wash and wipe 1 lb. of smooth, ripe tomatoes, and cut them in rather thick slices; put them into a buttered baking dish, sprinkle each layer with a little minced parsley, salt, pepper, a pinch of dry mustard, and a few drops of lemon juice or vinegar. Make a thin batter with 1 c. flour, 1 tsp. oil, a pinch of salt, 1 well-beaten egg, and a little water. Pour this over the tomatoes and bake in a moderate oven (350°F) until nicely browned. Serve in the same dish as soon as done; if an outside dish is not at hand, pin a large, white napkin about it.

❧ Cream of Tomato Soup
October 1910

Boil together 1 qt. ripe tomatoes, chopped; one small onion, sliced; and three or four cloves. Strain, add ½ tsp. salt, a little sugar and pepper, and ½ tsp. baking soda. Bring 1 qt. milk to a boil, then add 1 heaping tbsp. butter; stir in tomatoes. Do not allow to boil or soup will curdle.

TOMATO TIME
August 1935
Miriam J. Williams

When last we stopped at Aunt Martha's, she served a platter of scrambled eggs within a ring of broiled tomatoes and bacon. Compliments were plentiful.

As usual, Aunt Martha took it all gracefully with some remark about having been in a tomato time rut. Later, she told me that she had checked up privately to find that she had served plain sliced tomatoes twelve times in one week. "Tomatoes deserve more respect than that," was her comment.

❦ Tomatoes on Toast
August 1911

Peel ripe tomatoes and cut them in halves. Season with salt and pepper and put them in a buttered baking dish with a little bit of butter on each piece. Cover the tin with greased paper and let the tomatoes bake at 350°F for about 20 minutes. Lift them out carefully and place each half on a square or round of hot, buttered toast. Serve at once. If for breakfast, put a poached egg on top of each tomato half.

❦ Tomato Salad
September 1912

Scald, peel, and chill as many tomatoes as will be required. Cut them in halves and lay each half in a nest of crisp lettuce, cut side up. Mix together 1 tbsp. grated horseradish, 1 tbsp. lemon juice, a dash of cayenne, and ¼ tsp. salt. Stir this into 4 tbsp. cream, whipped stiff. Dust each piece of tomato with paprika and put 1 tbsp. dressing on each one.

❧ Cantaloupe as Dessert
August 1913

In the season of cantaloupe, one can have it filled with ice cream and various fruits when having it as dessert, but it is especially good when filled with cut-up peaches that have been sprinkled with sugar and a little Maraschino added.

❧ Peach Dumplings
September 1912

Make a rich biscuit dough:
Mix and sift 2 c. flour, 3 tsp. baking powder, and 1 tsp. salt; quickly work in 4 tbsp. fat with a fork or dough blender. Add ⅔ c. milk all at once and stir lightly to make a soft dough. Turn out onto a slightly floured board and knead lightly for a few seconds.

Roll thin and cut out saucer-size. Place in each one peach peeled and sliced, sprinkle with sugar and small pieces of butter, roll up, and pinch together securely at the top. Place in a deep pan with pieces of butter, sugar, and peach slices surrounding them, pour over all 1 c. boiling water, and place in the oven at 350°F at once. Bake for half an hour. When nicely browned, serve hot with sugar and cream.

❦ Peach Custard Pie

November 1911
Contributed by Mrs. Whitehouse

Fill the unbaked crust with sliced peaches. Pour in an ordinary custard mixture—1 c. milk cooked thick with ½ c. plus 1 tbsp. sugar and 2 tbsp. flour, two egg yolks beaten in slowly, then the mixture cooled—and bake at 325°F until the custard sets.

Meringue:
2 egg whites
2 tbsp. sugar
¼ tsp. vanilla

Beat the whites until stiff but not dry. Add sugar and beat until smooth and glossy. Add vanilla, spread on top of pie, and bake.

❦ Peach Soufflé

August 1928

Peach soufflé needs freshest, ripest fruit. Peel, stone, and fork pulp one dozen very ripe, very fresh peaches. Crush in with this two very ripe bananas, pared and scraped, blending the juice of two sweet oranges in with the whole. Then add the stiffly beaten yolks of one dozen eggs, beating thoroughly. Cook this over a brisk fire until puffing up highly, then stir in 1 pt. of thick, sweet cream. When thoroughly heated through, add 1 lb. of whole, fresh marshmallows. Let heat through again and add the quite stiffly beaten egg whites. Serve with whipped cream.

Plums are strong favorites with me because they add so much to a meal with their piquant flavor. In preparing plums recipes, one must sugar the fruit to suit the individual taste and use only the freshest, ripest fruit, for any suggestion of over- or under-ripeness quickly kills the plum's particular and delicious piquancy.

—The Farmer's Wife Magazine

❦ Plum Cream Pie
July 1929

Line deep tins with good flaky crust dough and fill them with very ripe peeled, seeded plums. Add a slight dusting of flour, a cup or so of sugar— according to the type of plum—a sprinkle of cinnamon, and *little*, if any, water; bake at 350°F until fruit is tender. Remove and cool and pile thick with sweetened whipped cream that is mixed with chipped marshmallows. This may be made of canned plums as well.

❦ Plum Salad
July 1929

Wash choice, ripe plums and polish dry. Split, remove seeds, and put on ice till shortly before serving. Arrange four halves on a bed of shredded lettuce on each salad plate. Stuff the cavities with cottage cheese slightly sweetened with Plum Salad Dressing (see below); then sprinkle chopped walnuts all over and serve with more dressing.

Plum Salad Dressing:
Obtain juice from the ripest, sweetest plums by simmering in a saucepan with a very little water for a few minutes. Remove from fire and strain through a thin, clean cloth. Add 1 tsp. cornstarch for each pt. of juice; sweeten to taste and boil 5 minutes.

September

Fortunate you are if your kitchen garden has given you a goodly supply of sweet peppers or pimientos, for there are always many delicious ways in which they may be served. The squat little pimiento is my favorite of the pepper family, so I mention it most frequently.

—The Farmer's Wife Magazine

❦ Stuffed and Baked Pimientos
September 1927

With a pointed knife remove a cap from the pimiento, setting it aside to be used later. Do not make the opening larger than necessary for removing the seeds. Make a filling of:

1½ c. ground ham or other meat
1½ c. dried breadcrumbs
½ c. milk
1 tsp. dry mustard
1 tsp. sugar
salt and pepper to taste

Mix all together and tightly stuff the pimientos, replacing the caps when filled. Arrange in a covered baking dish into which ¼ c. water has been added. Bake at 350°F till pimientos are tender, 30–45 minutes. These are excellent and are very good served cold the next day, providing there are any left.

Pimiento Relish
September 1927

3 doz. pimientos
15 onions
1½ c. sugar
3 tbsp. salt
1 qt. vinegar

Chop pimientos and onions quite fine, cover with boiling water, and let stand 5 minutes. Drain and add other ingredients. Cook 15 minutes and serve. This is a delicious relish and adds a pretty touch to the table when served. Leftovers may be stored in the refrigerator for up to a week.

Raw Carrot Salad
November 1924

2 c. carrot, grated
½ c. cabbage, chopped
1 tbsp. onion, chopped
salad dressing

This is even better than it looks! The salad dressing may be either mayonnaise, cooked, or French. ¾ c. grated cheese may be substituted for the cabbage.

❦ Cauliflower au Gratin

June 1922

Remove leaves and stalk from one large head of cauliflower and soak in cold, slightly salted water for 1 hour. Place in a kettle of boiling salted water and cook 30 minutes. (Sometimes to retain shape of head it is necessary to tie a square of cheesecloth over head.) Place whole cooked cauliflower in a shallow baking dish, sprinkle with grated cheese and Buttered Breadcrumbs (pg. 13), and brown in oven at 350°F for about 20 minutes. Remove from oven, pour 2 c. White Sauce (pg. 89) over cauliflower, and serve at table from baking dish.

In many farm homes, apples are one of the staple supplies stored for the winter time. Others are not so fortunate in having their own crop, and unthinkingly deprive themselves of an economical source of personal enjoyment and healthful food.

—The Farmer's Wife Magazine

❦ Apple and Celery Salad

October 1922

3 medium apples, pared and cubed
1 c. celery, cubed
¼ c. walnuts
1 c. Mayonnaise Dressing (pg. 181)

Toss all together. Serve on lettuce leaf on salad plates or garnish with celery leaves.

EASY DESSERTS MADE WITH APPLES
October 1912
Maude Meredith

The season of apples is at hand, and we all know the good old ways of eating them. Apples are so good that any way is good enough. The little tads who have all the bread and butter and apples they can eat, need no other lunches. The breakfast table that has a steaming platter of fried apples is good enough for a king. Fried apples and corn bread! Don't it "make your mouth water?" And the apples dumplings for dinner, and applesauce for supper.

But there are other days when we like to fix up some novelty. For such times I send a few fancy recipes that will be found excellent.

❦ Delicious Apple Dumplings
October 1910

These are easily and quickly made and always light and digestible. Pare and core ½ dozen medium-sized tart apples. Put on to cook with water to cover. Then beat one egg to a froth, add to this 3 tbsp sugar, 3 tbsp. milk, and a pinch of salt. Stir into this ¾ c. flour into which has been added 2 level tsp. baking powder. Drop in small portions into the cooking apples. Cover and cook slowly for 12 minutes, then remove to individual saucers and surround with apples. Serve with cream and sugar.

A Guide To Apple Varieties

Applesauce and pie

Duchess	Greening
Maiden Blush	Rome Beauty
Lady Blush	Wealthy

Stewed Apples and pie

Jonathan	Ontario
Northern Spy	Baldwin
McIntosh	Golden Pippin

Baking

Jonathan	Tolman Sweet
McIntosh	Golden Pippin
Ontario	Tompkins King
Baldwin	Hubbardston
Twenty Ounce	Rome Beauty

Dessert (eating from hand)

Jonathan	Russet	Winter Banana
McIntosh	Winesap	Stark's Delicious
Ontario	Cortland	Golden Delicious
Baldwin	Wealthy	Grimes Golden
Gravenstein		Yellow Newton
Northern Spy		Huntsman's Favorite

❦ Apple Snow
January 1911

Cut a sponge cake into very thin slices, using two for each serving. Fill with a mixture made by beating the whites of three eggs, adding 1 c. stewed apples and ½ c. sugar, and folding together. When the cake has been filled, cover the top with whipped cream and serve cold.

❦ Apple Frost
August 1913

Pare and core eight good-sized apples. Cut in small pieces and stand aside in enough cold water to cover. Put on the stove 1 qt. water and 1 c. sugar. Boil until sugar is dissolved, place apples in syrup, and cook until very tender. Mash through colander and stand aside till thoroughly cooled. Beat up the whites of two eggs and mix these with the apples. Put in freezer and freeze as you would ice cream. This makes a dainty dessert for a warm day.

❦ Compote of Apples
October 1912

Make a syrup with 1 c. sugar, 1 c. water, 1-inch stick cinnamon, and the juice of one lemon. Boil slowly for 5 minutes. Core and pare six apples and cook them in the syrup till almost done. Drain and finish by baking at 350°F for 10–20 minutes, till very soft. Boil syrup down to a jelly. Fill apple centers with whipped cream. Pour syrup around apples; sprinkle with chopped nuts and put whipped cream around base.

❦ Fried Apples
September 1913
With the first shower of "Early Harvest" scarcely large enough to peel, the luscious apple forms a part of our daily menu and is not to be slighted in any of the many ways it appears during the season.
                                              —The Farmer's Wife Magazine

Wash and slice apples with the peeling on. Brown ½ c. butter in a deep pan, put in the sliced apples, cover with sugar and water, and let stew until tender.

❦ Apple Cobbler
October 1929

4 c. sliced apples (6–8 apples)   ½ c. butter
½ c. water   1 pt. whipped cream
1 tsp. cinnamon   1 tsp. sugar
1 c. sugar
¾ c. flour

Cut apples in ¼-inch slices and place them in a buttered baking dish. Add water and cinnamon. Work together the sugar, flour, and butter until crumbly. Spread over apples and bake uncovered at 350°F. Serve hot with whipped cream, sweetened with sugar.

❦ Apple Brown Betty
October 1938

4 c. soft breadcrumbs
½ c. melted butter
4 c. sliced apples
juice of 1 lemon
½ tsp. grated lemon rind
½ tsp. cinnamon
1 c. sugar
¾ c. water
cream to serve

Moisten breadcrumbs with butter and place in baking dish, alternating with apples. Top with layer of crumbs. Sprinkle each layer with lemon juice and rind, cinnamon, and sugar. Pour water over top. Cover and bake at 350°F for 1 hour. Uncover last 15 minutes in order to brown. Serve hot with cream.

❦ Apple Injun
February 1925

3 c. milk
½ c. cornmeal
1 tsp. cinnamon
1 tsp. salt
1½ c. brown sugar
1 pt. cold milk
1 qt. sweet apples, cut in eighths

Scald 3 c. milk and sift in cornmeal, stirring rapidly. Cook 5 minutes. Remove from fire and add cinnamon, salt, sugar, milk, and apples cut in eighths. Bake slowly in a deep, covered dish at 325°F for 4 hours. Serve with ice cream.

❦ Apple Cake
May 1927

2½ c. flour
pinch of salt
1 tsp. baking powder
2 tbsp. butter or lard
1 c. milk
6 tart apples
sugar, cinnamon, unsalted butter

Mix in a dough and roll out to ½ inch thick. Line a square tin with dough to 1 inch from top. Pare, core, and quarter apples to fill in, standing apples on ends. Sprinkle with sugar, cinnamon, and bits of butter. Bake and serve as any cake (350°F, until cooked through).

❦ Applesauce
October 1938

2½ qts. peeled, sliced apples
¾ c. water
¾ c. sugar

Put the apples and the water into a saucepan, cover tightly, and cook rapidly without stirring until they begin to boil. The apples should be cooked to a mush by this time. Add the sugar and cook for 2 or 3 minutes longer, stirring constantly. More or less water may be used, depending on stiffness desired.

❦ Applesauce Cheese Tarts
October 1935

1 c. flour
¼ tsp. salt
⅓ c. butter
¼ c. grated cheddar cheese
2½ to 3 tbsp. ice water
Applesauce (see above)

Sift flour and salt together into mixing bowl; add butter and cut in with pastry blender or two knives until particles are size of wheat grains. Stir in grated cheese. Add water by teaspoonfuls, tossing with fork till all flour is moistened. Gather into a ball and divide into four or five portions (one for each tart). Shape into balls, flatten on floured board, and roll out to fit over bottoms of inverted tart or muffin tins. Trim and prick all over with a fork. Chill for 30 minutes, then bake at 425°F for 10–15 minutes, till slightly browned. Remove from pans and cool. When cold, heap chilled applesauce into the shells and garnish with grated cheese or stiffly whipped cream.

TABLE TALK
September 1914
Sarah A. Cooke

When the first strong wind starts to blow, the late, half-ripe summer apples begin to fall, and while they are not perfect enough to bake, they may be utilized in a hundred and one different ways in cookery. Besides making good pies, puddings, dumplings, or turnovers, these apples are excellent for making applesauce, and as the summer fruits are often still plentiful in the markets when the early apples begin to ripen, many delicious and healthful sauces are possible.

Applesauce, which is rather tart, forms a splendid substitute for pickles, mustard, or other unhealthful condiments when served with meat. A dessert served with cream, either plain or whipped, in place of pies or puddings, the sauce will always find favor.

Huckleberry Pudding
August 1913

A very inexpensive dessert can be made from huckleberries and leftover pieces of bread, which is good tasting enough to make one forget its economic origin. Roll out enough breadcrumbs to make 1 lb. and mix them with 2 tbsp. melted butter, then stir in 1 c. huckleberries. Mix together with two eggs and a little milk and put the batter into a steamer to cook for 1 hour. A double boiler serves very well to cook this in because when it is ready to serve, it can be turned out like a mold and served with either Hard Sauce (pg. 127) or a hot vanilla sauce.

To make the vanilla sauce beat one egg well and add to it 1 c. heating milk and 1 tbsp. sugar. Cook over medium-low flame until it begins to thicken, then take from the fire and add 1 tsp. vanilla extract when it is ready to serve.

October

With October comes Hallowe'en, and with Hallowe'en comes a desire to be festive, and with festivity comes feasting.

—The Farmer's Wife Magazine

❦ Beets and Greens with Sour Sauce
April 1926

2 bunches beets and greens	2 tbsp. flour
½ c. sugar	½ c. vinegar
salt	4 tbsp. butter

Cut the greens from the beets, leaving a 1-inch tail on the beets. Wash all thoroughly. Cook the beets in a very little water in a covered pot till almost tender; add the greens and cook till all are very tender. Add more water as necessary, 2 tbsp. at a time, to the pot as the beets cook. Cut the greens into pieces; peel and cut beets into cubes, leaving small beets whole. Mix sugar and flour, add vinegar slowly, and cook 5 minutes, stirring constantly. Add butter and stir to melt. Pour over greens, garnish with beets, and serve at once.

❦ Beets and Onion Supreme
September 1929

3 c. cooked beets	1 tbsp. sugar
1 medium onion	salt, pepper to taste
2 tbsp. butter	3 tbsp. fresh parsley, chopped
4 tbsp. vinegar	

Dice the beets and onion. Melt butter in saucepan and add all ingredients except parsley. Cook over slow fire for a few minutes. Add parsley just before serving.

❧ Stewed Cabbage
October 1920

Shred two heads of green cabbage. Cook in a large amount of salted water with the cover off, till just tender. (It will take about 15 minutes for young cabbage.) Season to taste with cream, salt, and pepper.

❧ Baked Cabbage
August 1929

2 c. shredded cabbage, parboiled for 2 minutes
1 tsp. salt
½ tsp. pepper
¾ c. breadcrumbs
1 tbsp. flour
1 c. milk
4 tbsp. grated Swiss cheese
2 tbsp. butter

Place a thin layer of cabbage in a baking dish; season, cover with a layer of breadcrumbs; repeat till dry ingredients are used, having the top layer of breadcrumbs. Pour on milk and sprinkle cheese and butter on top. Bake at 325°F, until top is nicely browned.

❧ Escalloped Eggplant with Tomatoes and Onions
August 1927

Peel and slice thin one large eggplant. In an oiled baking dish place alternate layers of eggplant and sliced ripe tomatoes, seasoning each layer with salt, butter, and a little chopped onion. Bake about 30 minutes at 350°F, till eggplant is tender.

❦ Cranberry and Raisin Pie

October 1930

Contributed by Mrs. E. M. T., Virginia

1½ c. cranberries
1 c. raisins
½ c. sugar
pie crusts

Chop cranberries, mix with raisins and sugar, and bake all in a shallow pan between two crusts.

Harvest Layer Cake

October 1933

3 c. sifted cake flour
3 tsp. baking powder
½ tsp. salt
½ c. butter
1¼ c. brown sugar, firmly packed
3 egg yolks, unbeaten
1 c. milk
1½ tsp. vanilla

Sift flour once, measure, add baking powder and salt, and sift together three times. Cream butter thoroughly, add sugar gradually, and cream together until light and fluffy. Add egg yolks; beat well. Add flour alternately with milk, a small amount at a time. Beat after each addition until smooth. Add vanilla. Bake in two greased 9-inch layer pans in moderate oven (375°F) for 30 minutes, or until done. Spread frosting between layers and on top and sides of cake. Sprinkle nuts over top and sides of cake while frosting is still soft, if desired. (*All measurements are level.*)

November

Each member of the rural home has had a share in producing the bountiful returns for which gratitude is outpoured. Is it not, therefore, entirely fitting that just so far as may be everyone of the thanksgivingers have a part in the preparation of the busy year's crowning feast?

—The Farmer's Wife Magazine

❦ Crème de Menthe Pears
November 1931

3 c. sugar
3 c. water
½ tsp. mint oil
12 firm pears, pared, cored, and halved

Make a syrup of the sugar and water by bringing to a boil over medium heat. Stir in mint oil. Drop pears into the hot syrup and cook until clear. Serve warm, with whipped cream or ice cream.

❦ Sweet Potato Puff
November 1924

6 sweet potatoes, pared and cut into cubes
2 tbsp. butter
½ tsp. salt
2 egg whites, stiffly beaten

Boil the potatoes till soft, then mash. Add butter, salt, and stiffly beaten egg whites. Fill buttered custard cups. Set in a pan of hot water and bake 20 minutes at 400°F. Serve hot, straight from the cups.

❦ Stuffed Sweet Potatoes
January 1911

Bake large, smooth sweet potatoes at 400°F until soft through, about
1 hour. When done, cut in half length-wise and remove from skins. Mash,
add ½ tbsp. butter per potato, salt and pepper to taste, and a drizzling of
heavy cream, beating thoroughly. Refill skins, set back in oven, and brown
before serving.

❦ Glaceéd Sweet Potatoes
November 1913

6 sweet potatoes
butter
sugar

Parboil sweet potatoes, then skin them and cut in half lengthwise (in
several pieces if very large). Place them in a baking tin, dab with bits of
butter, and sprinkle sugar over them very lightly. Bake at 350°F until sugar
is melted and browned, about 20 minutes, and turn each piece, buttering
and sugaring them as before. Put into the oven again for a few minutes and
serve very hot.

❦ Scalloped Sweet Potato and Apple
November 1923

Into a buttered baking dish put a ½-inch layer of pared, sliced sour apples.
Sprinkle with sugar. Cover with a layer of pared, sliced sweet potatoes,
season with salt and pepper, dot with butter, and sprinkle generously with
sugar. Repeat, having not more than three layers. Cover for the first 15
minutes of baking at 375°F, then bake uncovered until the apples are
soft—45–60 minutes.

❧ Pumpkin Butter
November 1912

1 medium-sized pumpkin (2–3 lbs.)
sugar
ground ginger

Cut pumpkin into pieces, removing the rind and seeds. Place it in a large pan with an equal measure of sugar, 1 oz. of ground ginger for each 2 lbs. pumpkin, and enough water to cover. Boil until very thick, stirring often so it does not burn. Skim off the froth and remove from heat. Store in refrigerator and use, as a spread for toast or waffles, within 1 week.

❧ Pumpkin Pie Filling
November 1922
This recipe is taken from Pearl L. Bailey's Domestic Science Principles and Application *(Webb Publishing Company, St. Paul). The recipe makes one pie. Ten pies will serve 50.*

1½ c. cooked and strained pumpkin
⅔ c. brown sugar
1 tsp. salt
½ tsp. ground ginger or nutmeg
1 tsp. cinnamon
1½ c. milk
12 eggs, slightly beaten
1 tsp. orange juice
pie crust

Mix pumpkin, sugar, salt, and spices. Add milk and eggs slightly beaten. Beat well, then add orange juice. Fill crust and bake 10 minutes at 425°F. Lower heat to 300°F and continue baking 45 minutes, or until custard is firm.

Roast Turkey
November 1938

Stuff and truss bird. Rub surface with soft fat. Place on a rack in an open roaster, breast side down, turning first on one side, then the other during roasting. Bake uncovered in a very moderate oven (300–350°F). If the bird gets too brown, cover with a clean white cloth dipped in fat. Allow 20–25 minutes per pound (dressed but undrawn weight) for a small bird (8–10 lbs.); 18–20 minutes per pound for a medium bird (10–16 lbs.); and 15–18 minutes per pound for a large bird (18–25 lbs.). A test for doneness is a loose leg joint when the drumstick is twisted.

Turkey Stuffing
November 1915

1 qt. coarse breadcrumbs	2 tbsp. poultry spice
½ c. salt pork, chopped, or butter	pepper to taste
2 tsp. salt	milk or water

Mix all together, moistening slightly with the milk or water. Chestnuts shelled, skinned, and cooked tender are often added. Sausage meat is sometimes used with an equal measure of crumbs.

Lazy Day Late Summer Picnics

The farmer's wife and her family loved a picnic as much as your family no doubt does. Not surprisingly, she had a slew of ideas about which foods to prepare for such an outing.

MAKE IT A PICNIC

| AFTER A LONG AUTO TRIP | Picnic Pie   Mustard Pickles
Fresh Sliced Tomatoes
Buttered Rolls   Conserve
Mother's Sour Cream Doughnuts
Quick Camp Coffee   Fruit | |

| | One-Pot Meal   Toasted Buns
Celery, Olives, Pickles
Molasses Cream Cake
Cocoa or Coffee | FOOL-PROOF and FUN |

| FAMILY PICNIC OLD STYLE | Two-Tone Meat Loaf
Country Kitchen Potato Salad
Dark and Light Bread Sandwiches
Ice Cream   Cookies or Cake
Independence Day Punch | |

OUT-OF-DOOR LUNCHEONS FOR SUMMER
July 1914
Sarah A. Cooke

Nothing furnishes more genuine enjoyment than a luncheon eaten in the open air. There is something stimulating and exhilarating in the atmosphere one breathes outside of houses. Whatever this element is, it acts as a tonic and will make the most indifferent appetite rally nobly. Picnic or camp fare is almost always eaten voraciously.

Eat out of doors as frequently as possible. The outdoor luncheon should be an occasion for relaxation and amusement. Hence, it is of prime importance that the labor of preparing the picnic meal be reduced to a minimum.

If much work is required, the idea of the luncheon in the open is associated with drudgery instead of pleasure. If the housewife has toiled

in the preparation of a menu until she is weary, she is, at the outset, in no frame of mind to enjoy what would otherwise be a season of contentment and a time of recuperation for mind and body. Besides this, no woman who has fretted regarding the success of attempts at making intricate pastry and difficult or delicate cakes particularly relishes the productions after they are ready to be consumed.

Those who dine out of doors frequently are in the habit of making use of the paper napkins, plates, and cups that nowadays may be purchased so cheaply of almost any dealer. No other dishes are needed with the exception of a few spoons, knives, and forks; but even these may be left at home.

As to the bill of fare, fruit is always acceptable. So are hard-boiled eggs, which may be served in a variety of ways. Bread or buns are good, and may be served alone or made into sandwiches with eggs or cheese. Peanut butter is very highly prized by many veterans in the army of outdoor dinners. Potato salad and baked beans are popular with those who insist on vegetables. Pickles of all kinds are held in high esteem for the picnic lunch.

Nearly everyone will devour radishes greedily. Jelly in screw-top glass receptacles adds a touch of variety, and honey may give a pleasing finish to the meal eaten in the open air. Cookies are good, and so are crackers. Simple cake may be carried, but care should be taken to avoid anything along this line that will crush easily or become "messy."

As to what one should drink—water is the most popular fluid with the usual picnicker. It is always best to serve the outdoor luncheon in close proximity to a bountiful source of good, cold drinking water. Some lunch baskets always contain cold tea, while some housewives have formed the habit of carrying lemon juice, well-sweetened, in a screw-top receptacle or tightly-corked bottle. This makes the preparation of lemonade a decidedly simple matter.

These are but suggestions as to satisfactory rations for an ordinary meal outside the house. The average housewife will make many pleasing variations and combinations. But as stated before, when the luncheon is most simply prepared with the least possible amount of labor, it is generally most satisfactory. When the meal is ended, if dishes and napkins can be cast aside, the dish-washing problem is happily solved and a new feature of freedom from responsibility is added to the expedition.

Picnic Nibbles

What to eat while you swim, loll, chat, and laze.

❦ Deviled Eggs
July 1914

4 hard-cooked eggs
¼ tsp. salt
½ tsp. Dijon mustard
⅛ tsp. pepper

1 tsp. vinegar
2 tsp. mayonnaise
paprika

Remove shells from eggs and cut in half lengthwise. Remove the yolks and mash them smooth with all remaining ingredients except paprika. Roll mixture into eight balls and place back in each half of egg. Garnish with sprinkle of paprika.

❦ Easy Fattigmands
July 1932

1 whole egg
5 egg yolks
6 tbsp. sugar
6 tbsp. whipping cream
1¾ c. flour
1 tsp. vanilla extract

Beat egg and yolks until light, add sugar, then beat again. Whip cream and add to eggs. Add flour and flavoring and mix well. Roll extremely thin, then cut in diamond shapes. Make slit in one point and slip end through. Fry in hot lard (they fry very fast)—about four at a time is enough. Turn as they come up and take out. Drain on brown paper or paper towels. Sprinkle with powdered sugar if you desire.

❧ Marguerites
May 1933
Contributed by Mrs. B.W., Massachusetts

2 egg whites
3 tbsp. raspberry or other jam
½ c. chopped nuts
2 drops lemon extract
10 to 15 crackers, such as Ritz

Beat egg whites stiff and gradually add the jam and beat until thoroughly blended. Add 1 tbsp. of chopped nuts and flavoring. Place a spoonful of the mixture on a cracker and sprinkle with chopped nuts. Bake in a hot oven (400°F) until delicately brown.

❧ Honey Apricot Straws
August 1933

Use pie crust and work in as much Honey Apricot Spread (see below) as possible. Run through cookie tube to form little straws. Bake at 375°F for 15 minutes.

Honey Apricot Spread:
Grind up 1 c. dried apricots with 1½ c. honey in a blender.

Cheese Straws
February 1917

¼ lb. butter
¼ lb. flour
¼ lb. grated cheddar cheese
½ tsp. salt
cayenne
milk to moisten

Cream the butter and rub into the flour. Add the grated cheese and enough milk to moisten for kneading. Knead all ingredients until smooth and roll out on a floured board to ¼ inch thick. Mark off carefully into strips 4 inches long and ¼ inch wide. Bake carefully in an ungreased pan at 400°F until light brown.

Bread Sticks
December 1919

Cut stale bread in strips 4 or 5 inches long and ½ inch wide. Spread with melted butter and brown in the oven.

❦ Ginger Snaps
June 1921

1 c. sugar
1 c. butter
1 c. molasses
1 tbsp. baking soda
1 egg
1 tbsp. ground ginger
6 c. flour
1 tbsp. vinegar

Mix sugar, butter, molasses, and vinegar thoroughly. Add baking soda and egg and beat well. Sift the ginger with 3 c. flour and beat well. Add remainder of flour, knead into shape, and set in a cold place for 1 hour till chilled. Roll thin and bake on buttered sheets at 350°F.

The dough is very stiff after adding last flour. No flour is needed when rolling preparatory to cutting cookies.

❦ Easy Chocolate Cookies
September 1938

1 egg
1 c. sugar
½ c. melted butter
½ c. milk
1 tsp. vanilla
2 c. flour

3 tbsp. cocoa powder
½ tsp. baking soda
½ tsp. baking powder
¼ tsp. salt
½ c. raisins

Beat egg, sugar, and butter together. Add milk and vanilla, sifted dry ingredients, and raisins. Drop on a greased cookie sheet and bake 20 minutes at 400°F.

❦ Date Bars
1934

⅔ c. flour
¼ tsp. salt
½ tsp. baking powder
2 c. sliced dates
1 c. shredded unsweetened cocoanut
2 eggs
½ c. sugar
powdered sugar

Sift dry ingredients and add dates and cocoanut to dredge. Beat eggs till light, then add sugar and mix well. Add to flour and fruit and mix well. Spread thin in buttered sheet pans and bake 40 minutes at 325°F. Cool slightly, then cut in strips and roll in powdered sugar.

❦ Peanut Butter Bread
November 1934

2 c. bread flour
⅓ c. sugar
2 tsp. baking powder
1 tsp. salt
¾ c. peanut butter
1 egg, beaten
1 c. milk

Sift dry ingredients together. Work in peanut butter with a fork, adding egg and milk to make a soft dough. Pour in a greased loaf pan. Bake at 375°F for 50–60 minutes.

Sandwiches

Sandwiches are an important part of the picnic luncheon. They may be better prepared in advance and wrapped separately in waxed paper; then again it may be more convenient to carry the loaf of bread, a sharp knife, and a jar of prepared sandwich filling and put them together as needed. Mix butter and seasoning with the filling, spread one slice of bread, and press another on that and the sandwich is ready.

—The Farmer's Wife Magazine

RULES FOR MAKING SANDWICHES
October 1924

The sandwich forms the basis of the cold lunch. Usually two thin slices of bread, buttered and put together with a filling, are more to be desired than thick buns, although a bun hollowed out and filled with salad or sandwich filling is very good.

Here are five points to be observed in sandwich making:

1. Bread must be well baked and if 24-hours old will make a neater sandwich. Give less of white bread than whole wheat, graham, rye, brown bread, or oatmeal bread. Nut bread, raisin bread, and orange bread make delicious sandwiches just with butter.
2. Butter should be creamed, not melted, to make it spread evenly. It destroys the appetite to bite into chunks of butter.
3. Seldom use all sandwiches of one kind. Use two of one kind (meat, eggs, fish) to one of sweet filling such as marmalade or jelly.
4. Each sandwich should be wrapped separately in waxed paper to keep from drying and to keep clean.
5. For the growing child, crusts are beneficial, but for a "fancy" or special treat sandwich they may be removed.

❦ Tomato Sandwich
July 1912

Peel raw tomatoes, remove the seed and mince the remaining pulp, season with salt and pepper, thicken with fine cracker crumbs, add a minced onion if liked (or mayonnaise), and spread between slices of stale bread.

Bread for sandwiches is nice if baked in pound baking-powder boxes; bake with the lid on and there will be no hard crusts, and the sandwiches will be dainty and just the right size.

❦ Chicken Sandwich
July 1912

Mince fine some boiled chicken. Put in a saucepan with enough water to soften. Boil until thick, adding salt and pepper to taste when it begins to boil. When thick remove from the fire and turn onto a plate to cool, then when cold slice thin and place between slices of buttered bread.

❦ Vegetable Sandwich Filling
March 1928

1 c. sugar
4 tbsp. flour
1 tsp. ground mustard
2 tsp. salt
4 medium onions
12 medium red peppers
1½ c. vinegar
½ c. water

Thoroughly mix together the sugar, flour, mustard, and salt. Finely mince with peppers and onions, then drain off liquid. Mix all ingredients together, cook 20 minutes, and allow to cool before spreading on bread or toast.

❦ Egg Sandwiches
July 1914

Hard boil four eggs and add four sour pickles minced fine. Moisten all with mayonnaise. Spread between slices of buttered brown bread.

❦ Sandwich Filling
July 1913
Contributed by Mary Rutlenge

Lettuce and Onion:
Chop lettuce and young onions rather fine, add chopped hard-boiled egg, salt, pepper, a pinch of dry mustard, and a small amount of vinegar for a filling sandwich. Mayonnaise may be used for the seasoning if desired.

Radish Sandwich:
Chop crisp radishes fine, then add salt with a little pepper. Spread on well-buttered, thin slices of bread.

Cucumber Sandwiches:
Slice the cucumber very thin, soak ½ hour in salt water, dry the slices, then dip in a thick, creamy salad dressing. Place these with a lettuce leaf between pieces of bread which have been lightly buttered.

Chopped Ham Filling:
Cold boiled ham chopped fine with lettuce and hard-boiled egg is good when mixed with mayonnaise. Cold boiled ham and mayonnaise spread on the bread, then stuffed olives sliced over it before adding the other slice of bread is fine. Cold boiled beef or chicken may be used instead of ham.

Salmon Sandwiches:
Chop cabbage very fine. Stir into salmon which has been well broken up, and add salt, pepper, and enough lemon juice to make rather sour.

Fruit and Nut Sandwiches:
Chop raisins, figs, and English walnuts together. Add enough sweet cream to make the mixture spread well. Put between slices of graham bread.

Plain Lettuce Sandwiches:
[Iceberg] lettuce soaked in salt water for 1 hour then placed between thin, lightly buttered slices of white bread, spread very lightly with mayonnaise, makes a delicate sandwich.

Waldorf Filling:
Finely chopped apples, walnuts, and mayonnaise form the Waldorf filling.

Whipped Cream Filling:
Whipped cream with chopped nuts is delicious. Also, either banana or grated pineapple with the whipped cream may be used, or the whipped cream may be placed between thin slices of bread which have been spread lightly with raspberry or strawberry jam. Whipped cream filling must not be put into sandwiches until just ready to serve.

Cheese and Pimento:
Beat a large chopped pimento into a small brick of cream cheese, and an excellent sandwich filling will result. If too stiff, add a very small amount of cream.

❧ Some More Sandwich Fillings

October 1938

Hard-cooked eggs and mango
Carrots and raisins
Baked beans moistened with mustard or catsup

"Sandwich Filling":
6 mangos
1 medium head cabbage
6 small onions
2½ c. vinegar
2 c. sugar
2 tbsp. celery seed
2 tbsp. white mustard seed

Chop all till fine. Add other ingredients and spread between bread layers.

❧ Cooked Raisin Filling

October 1924

1 c. chopped raisins
½ c. sugar
½ c. water
1 tsp. flour

Cook in double boiler till thick. Cool before spreading.

❦ Olive Sandwiches
July 1914

Stone and chop fine twenty-four olives, into which mix 1 c. mayonnaise. Butter thin slices of brown bread, spread with the olive filling, and make into sandwiches.

■■■

❦ Olive Sandwich Filling
March 1928

¼ c. sugar
1 tsp. salt
¼ tsp. red pepper
1 tsp. dry mustard
6 tbsp. flour
4 eggs yolks, beaten
1 c. cream
1 c. vinegar
1 c. water
3 tbsp. melted butter
6 medium sweet or dill pickles
1 c. olives

Thoroughly mix together the sugar, salt, pepper, mustard, and flour. Add to beaten egg yolks and beat again till blended. Add the cream and butter, and beat again. Heat the vinegar and water in a non-reactive pan, then gradually add to the first mixture, stirring all the while. Cook till thick, stirring constantly. Remove from the fire and when cold stir in the pickles and olives, which have been wiped very dry with a clean white cloth then finely diced. Pour the mixture into a glass fruit jar and keep in a cool place until needed.

TABLE TALK
WHY NOT HAVE A PICNIC OR
OUTDOOR LUNCHEON EACH WEEK?

August 1915

Anna Barrows

Where several households join in a picnic, labor may be lessened by arranging in advance that each be responsible for one article and only one. If Mrs. A. provides sandwiches, Mrs. B. a sweet, Mrs. C. the coffee or other beverage, Mrs. D. some fruit, and Mrs. E. a relish, there is little labor for any one. Even if only one family is concerned, a little thought will make things easy.

A picnic cupboard is a great help. In it should be kept odd dishes of no value, glass jars in which food products have come, paper or wooden dishes, paraffin, paper drinking cups, and so forth.

Plan to do as much as possible where the meal is to be eaten. A campfire is always a great attraction if it can be had with safety and put out before leaving. Little children, or those who do not enjoy such tasks at home, where they mean work and not play, may master cookery in this way.

❦ Denver Sandwiches
February 1923

1 c. cold boiled ham
1 small onion
1 dill pickle
1 egg

Chop ham, onion, and pickle fine and mix with the well-beaten egg. Toast twelve slices of bread and butter them. Put the ham mixture between the slices and trim. Serve hot with sliced dill pickles for garnish.

❦ Date and Nut Bread with Cream Cheese Filling
June 1921

Use thinly sliced date-nut bread. Spread with a filling made by grinding ¼ lb. cream cheese and ¼ lb. butter together till smooth and creamy, then adding one sweet green pepper which has been chopped. Spread generously, this makes an excellent sandwich.

❧ Peanut Butter Fillings

September 1936

To keep peanut butter from being stick-to-the-roof-of-your-mouth, blend it with cold water, the syrup from pickled peaches or apples, or fruit juice. It will take a surprising amount of liquid, and need only a little salt to make a palatable filling.

—The Farmer's Wife Magazine

Variations which are good:

With crisp bacon: Spread blended peanut butter generously on one slice of bread and creamery butter on the other. Sprinkle crisp, crumbled bacon between.

With pineapple: Blend peanut butter with crushed pineapple, using enough juice to make it spread easily. Add a dash of salt before spreading.

With banana: Blend peanut butter with lemon juice and a little water (or pickle juice) till smooth. Spread on both slices of bread and between put thinly sliced banana, or banana mashed with a fork till creamy.

❧ Sweet Chocolate Sandwiches

September 1929

2 oz. bittersweet chocolate
2 tbsp. unsweetened butter
1 c. powdered sugar
3 tbsp. heavy cream
⅔ c. finely chopped walnuts

Melt the chocolate in a double boiler; add butter, sugar, and cream and cook gently for 5 minutes. Add nuts. Cool slightly and spread between buttered slices of bread.

❦ Cottage Cheese Fillings
September 1936

Mash cottage cheese with a fork and mix with cream till thick and smooth. Blend with:

Crushed pineapple or apricot or orange marmalade. Spread on buttered bread. Put wafer-thin slices of cucumber between.

Peanuts or other nuts, chopped or ground, or blended peanut butter. Combine well with cottage cheese. Season with salt and paprika.

Vegetables and cottage cheese make attractive fillings. Chopped watercress or mint, or a very light scraping of onion and shredded carrots, or chopped celery and nuts are all good combined with cheese. Thinly sliced cucumber is very tasty. Spread one slice of bread with cheese, the other with salad dressing, and put vegetables between.

Crisp bacon and grated horseradish mixed with cottage cheese is an interesting combination.

Salads

Take a few along to accompany the sandwiches; or on a hot day, make do with a few salads on their own.

SEASONABLE SALADS
THEY ARE APPETIZING,
NOURISHING AND ECONOMICAL.
WHY NOT SERVE THEM?
April 1917
Pearl Bailey Lyons

Housewives too often neglect to give salads the proper place in the diet, serving them on special occasions. In reality the salad plays a very important part in the diet, and the wise planner will see that it is served in some form nearly every day.

Only fresh, crisp greens should be used. They should be washed, rolled in a wet cloth, and kept in a cold place for several hours before using. Ingredients, such as vegetables, fruits, or meat must be cut into uniformly sized pieces.

For a delicious country supper, serve vegetable salad or fish salad with baking powder biscuits, fruit, and coffee. To make fish salad, use our chicken salad recipe, substituting fish for chicken meat.

You have fresh foods a-plenty for varying the salads served this time of year, but are you familiar with the many different dressings which you can make to accompany them?

—The Farmer's Wife Magazine

❧ French Salad Dressing
April 1917

2 tbsp. vinegar
6 tbsp. oil
½ tsp. salt
¼ tsp. pepper
paprika

Combine ingredients in a bowl. Beat steadily until thoroly blended and thick.
Serve on fresh greens. The ingredients may be mixed, beaten, and put in a
bottle. Just before using, shake the bottle hard, thoroly, to blend the ingredients.

❧ Mayonnaise Dressing
April 1917

1 tsp. salt
¼ tsp. white pepper
2 egg yolks
2 c. olive oil
4 tbsp. vinegar or lemon juice
cayenne or paprika

Mix in a bowl which is ice cold, using a silver fork or flexible knife. Have all
the ingredients very cold. Mix the dry ingredients, add the slightly beaten
yolks in the bowl, then add the oil, drop by drop, beating constantly as it
is added. As the mixture thickens, add a few drops of the acid. When ¼ c.
oil has been used, add the oil by spoonfuls. Beat hard. The beating makes
the dressing stiff, and the oil makes it a permanent emulsion. If the mixture
curdles, add it slowly to a fresh yolk.

Thousand Island Dressing

April 1917

1 c. mayonnaise
2 tbsp. parsley, minced
2 tbsp. pimento, minced
2 tbsp. capers, minced
1 tbsp. onion, minced
2 tbsp. beets, minced

Add the finely minced ingredients to the mayonnaise. Mix well.

Sour Cream Dressing

June 1938

½ c. sugar
1 tsp. salt
¼ tsp. white pepper
2 tsp. Dijon mustard
3 tbsp. flour
1 c. sour cream
½ c. white vinegar or lemon juice
½ c. water

Combine dry ingredients in top of double boiler, blending well. Add sour cream, vinegar, and water; blend well and cook over hot water till smooth and thick. If not used at once, as on potato salad, stir occasionally while cooling and store in glass jar in refrigerator.

✿ Cabbage Salad
August 1916

½ head white cabbage
2 chopped hard-boiled eggs
1 cucumber, peeled and diced
3 slices white onion, minced
1 tbsp. chopped parsley

Dressing:
3 egg yolks
¼ c. sugar
2 tbsp. flour
1 tsp. dry mustard
1 tsp. salt
½ tsp. paprika
½ c. vinegar
1 tbsp. butter
1 c. sour cream

Add all the salad ingredients together and moisten with dressing prepared as follows: beat the yolks with the sugar and add the flour, mustard, salt, paprika, and vinegar. Cook in the upper part of the double boiler until well thickened, stirring constantly; then add the butter and when the dressing cools, fold in the sour cream. Chill the salad thoroly before serving.

❦ Cold Slaw

November 1910
Contributed by Mrs. M.C.A., Decou, Minnesota

Select a firm, white head of cabbage. Chop fine. Add a stalk of celery chopped fine or 1 tsp. celery seed instead. Add salt and pepper to taste and 1 tsp. vinegar. This seasons the cabbage and softens the celery. Add mayonnaise dressing: ¼–½ c. mayonnaise mixed with 2 tbsp. olive oil and 2 tbsp. Dijon mustard Salt and pepper to taste—just before serving.

❦ Vegetable Salad

April 1917

½ c. peas, cooked
½ c. carrots
½ c. corn kernels
beets or celery
French dressing

Combine these or any other leftover vegetables, chopped into small pieces. Season with French Salad Dressing (pg. 181).

☙ Country Kitchen Salad
July 1936

1 qt. cold, cooked cubed potatoes
1 tbsp. vinegar
1 tsp. salt
dash pepper and cayenne
¼ tsp. paprika
2 tbsp. oil
1 or 2 c. chopped celery, shredded lettuce, cucumber, sliced radishes
2 tbsp. chopped onion
4 hard-cooked eggs cut in eighths
½ c. chopped sweet pickle
2 c. salad dressing

Marinate cubed potatoes in vinegar, seasonings, and oil about 1 hour. Add the other ingredients. Blend with dressing. Part of the dressing may be mayonnaise, if desired. Salad is improved by standing, except for lettuce, which should not be added till just before serving.

Variations:
With carrots: Add ½–¾ c. finely shredded carrots to the dressing, omitting some of the other vegetables.

Marinating with sour cream: Omit oil, and instead heat ½ c. sour cream with vinegar and seasonings. Pour over potatoes and let stand until cold before mixing with other ingredients.

❦ Shredded Carrot Salad
1934

To 2 c. shredded carrots add any of the following:

½ c. chopped peanuts
½ c. grated cocoanut
1 c. shredded pineapple
2 diced oranges and 4 chopped marshmallows
½ c. chopped scallion
1 c. diced celery
1 c. chopped apple and ½ c. slivered almonds
⅔ c. raisins

Mix and serve with favorite salad dressing.

❦ Chicken Salad
April 1917

1½ c. cold boiled chicken
½ c. French Salad Dressing (pg. 181)
1½ c. chopped celery
Mayonnaise Dressing (pg. 181)

Cut chicken into 1-inch pieces and mix carefully with some French Salad Dressing. Let stand 1 hour. This process is called marinating. Add the celery to the chicken. Just before serving, mixed with some Mayonnaise Dressing.

❦ Apple Salad
October 1912

Select six perfect apples (bright red ones preferred). Cut a slice off stem end and remove pulp in as large pieces as possible, taking care not to break the skin so that when the apple is hollowed it can be used as a cup. Cut up the pulp in small cubes and mix with 2 c. celery cut in like-sized pieces, ½ c. chopped nuts, and salad dressing. Fill apples, cover with slices cut from the ends, and serve.

❦ Fruit Salad
April 1917

½ c. pineapple
½ c. orange segments
¼ c. cherries
¼ c. walnuts
½ c. heavy cream
¼ c. sugar

Cut the pineapple and oranges in pieces of convenient size and cut the cherries in half, discarding the pits. Also cut walnuts in pieces. Combine ingredients and let stand, toss lightly with cream and sugar just before serving.

❧ Grapefruit Salad

October 1931

Contributed by Miss Frances Dunning, Cafeteria Director, University Farm, St. Paul, Minnesota

2 grapefruit, peeled and broken into segments

½ c. diced celery
1 green pepper, sliced

Arrange on plates and serve with:

Thick French Dressing:

1 tsp. onion, minced
2 tsp. salt
2 tsp. ground mustard
1¼ tsp. paprika

⅓ c. vinegar
1 c. sugar
1 c. olive oil

Mix together well.

❧ German Potato Salad

February 1928

2 lbs. potatoes
salt
¾ lb. bacon
2 medium onions, sliced
½ c. vinegar
1 c. water
½ c. sugar

Boil potatoes without peeling. Drain, cool, peel, and chop. Salt lightly. Cut bacon into pieces and fry, then drain on paper. Cook onions in bacon fat till translucent. Add vinegar, water, and sugar. Stir to mix, bring to a boil, then add potatoes. Serve topped with bacon.

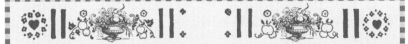

LET'S HAVE PICNIC SUPPERS BY A LITTLE PLANNING WE MAY HAVE THESE TREATS OFTEN

June 1919

Pearl Bailey Lyons

First let us plan to have on hand a supply of necessary equipment. This includes a good-sized, substantial basket—if you are to drive to the woods-nook or by-the-stream-place where you like to gather. Cardboard show boxes are ideal for carrying small items. If you need to get water from a spring or river, you will have to have a pail and dipper or a smaller pail with a stout string with which to let it down in the water. You will think of all these things; the point is to have them thought out beforehand and kept clean and ready where you can get at them instantly. A picnic list, written on the wall, is good.

For these picnic suppers, ask Mother to let you have an emergency shelf. [On it], keep a supply of things like these: potted meat, sardines, salmon, dried herring, dried beef, peanut butter (make this yourself), baked beans, canned corn, and canned tomatoes (these Mother has on hand in the cellar), pickles, sweet and sour, olives, and of course Mother will let you dip into her jams and jellies.

Here is a list of perishables, any of which are welcome at a picnic supper: lemons, fresh fruit, salad dressing (make a quart on some rainy day when you have to stay home, and put it in the ice box), cookies, cake, "weenies," beefsteak, ham, bacon, cheese, eggs, radishes, lettuce, green corn (in season), young onions, all are "found on the farm." So are cream, sweet and sour, whipped and unwhipped, and plenty of good butter. Berries, in season, can be picked the night before and put into jars with sugar.

With a little practice, you will soon be able to prepare nearly everything over your open campfire that you can cook at home on the stove-top. Potatoes may be baked in hot ashes or fried in the pan. Eggs cooked with bacon make fine hot sandwiches. Green corn on the cob is delicious roasted at the campfire or boiled. Spring chicken, sausage, and other meats are delicious when prepared in the long-handled frying pan, and steak or bacon can be broiled. Or hot meats may be entirely dispensed with.

I hope many of us will make this a summer of outdoor living. You cannot do this too often.

Picnic Eats for a Crowd
June 1924

Every alive community has its get-together days when, as one family, the whole group plays together. The day of days seems to be Picnic Day. Instead of each family working independently, why not have the women get together and decide on a menu, estimate as nearly as possible the amount needed, and then assign the foods to the various families?

Three Suggestive Menus

1.	2.	3.
Hot wieners	Sliced meat	Sandwiches
Rolls	Buttered rolls	Potato salad
Vegetable salad	Vegetable salad	Vegetable salad
Fruit	Potato salad	Pie
Cup cakes	Fruit	Pickles
Doughnuts	Pickles	Fruit
Pickles	Sheet cake	Lemonade
Coffee	Cookies	Coffee
Lemonade	Coffee	

Fruit Sandwiches for 25

1 lb. raisins
½ lb. figs
1½ c. sugar
1 tbsp. flour
¼ c. cold water
½ c. orange juice
rind and juice of 2 lemons

Chop the raisins and figs, then combine with sugar and flour. Add water and fruit juice and cook in a double boiler until thick. Use two full slices of bread for each sandwich.

Ham Sandwiches for 25

1 lb. cooked ham
⅔ c. chopped pickle
1 c. sifted breadcrumbs
1 c. salad dressing

Mix all together, using two full slices of bread for each sandwich.

Egg Sandwich Filling for 25

24 hard-boiled eggs
1 c. sifted breadcrumbs
1½ tbsp. lemon juice
2 tsp. salt
salad dressing

Chop eggs, add crumbs and seasoning, and make into a paste with the salad dressing.

Cabbage Salad for 60

4 lbs. cabbage
½ c. chopped pimientos
1½ c. chopped pickle
3 c. salad dressing

Vegetable Salad for 60

6 qts. boiled, diced potatoes
1 qt. diced cucumbers
2 qts. cut celery
2 c. chopped onion
up to 5 tbsp. salt
2 tsp. pepper
dressing (about 4 c.)

❦ One-Pot Meal

July 1936

1 lb. cured ham cut in ½-inch pieces
1 lb. bacon cut in 1-inch pieces
1 onion, chopped fine
2 tomatoes, chopped fine
1 c. corn kernels
1 c. frozen lima beans, parboiled to thaw
2 c. cooked macaroni
1 c. water

Placed the diced meat and onion in a heavy pot or frying pan and cook slowly till slightly browned and almost all the fat is fried out of the bacon. Add rest of ingredients along with water. Stir till mixed. Cook to heat through. Serve hot with crackers or bread toasted over the campfire.

❦ Picnic Pie

July 1936

1 onion, sliced
2 tbsp. drippings
1 lb. smoked ham
2 lbs. beef or veal
½ c. flour
2 pigs' feet
salt, pepper, dash of cayenne
3 c. cold water
pastry
3 hard-cooked eggs

Cook onion slices in drippings till light brown. Cut the ham and beef or veal in small pieces and dredge with flour. Fry with the onion until slightly brown. Put in saucepan with the pigs' feet and simmer till tender with water to just cover and seasonings. Strain from stock and combine with tender meat of pigs' feet. Cool. Line a loose-bottom cake tin with the pie dough, rolled ¼ inch thick. Half fill with meat and slice over this the hard-cooked eggs. Add remaining meat. Moisten all with about ½ c. stock. Cover with dough the same thickness as the bottom and sides, making slits in the top. Bake at 475°F for 15 minutes, then reduce heat to 350°F and bake 35 minutes longer. Remove from oven, cool somewhat, and pour remaining stock through slits in top. Cool thoroughly. The pie may be prepared a day ahead, kept in the icebox, and is fine for a long trip as it stands rough handling. Cut in pie-shaped wedges and serve with mustard or any hot sauce.

❦ Two-Tone Meatloaf
July 1936

Part I	Part II
1 lb. ground veal	1 lb. ground fresh pork
¾ lb. ground fat pork	½ lb. ground cured ham
3 crackers rolled into crumbs	2 eggs, beaten
1 tbsp. onion, chopped	½ c. breadcrumbs
½ tbsp. lemon juice	½ c. catsup
2 tbsp. cream	½ tsp. salt
salt and pepper to taste	dash pepper

Combine each set of loaf materials separately, mixing very thoroughly. Mold the first mixture into a firm oval loaf, and over it put the second mixture in an even layer. Place on a sheet of parchment or wax paper and set on a rack in an open roasting or dripping pan. Bake uncovered at 325°F for 2 hours. Makes a 3-lb. loaf.

❦ Salmon Loaf
1934

½ c. milk
¾ c. breadcrumbs
1 7 or 7½-oz. can salmon
2 eggs, beaten
2 tbsp. melted butter
juice of ½ lemon
salt and pepper

Heat milk and stir in breadcrumbs to make a paste. Add this to the salmon along with beaten eggs and seasonings. Put in well-buttered baking dish and bake at 400°F for 35 minutes.

For a Picnic Meal:
Salmon Loaf (cold)
Scalloped Corn
Fresh Garden Salad
Bread and Butter Sandwiches
Jelly
Sour Cream Chocolate Cake
Lemonade

One of the joys of the Fourth of July on the farm is the picnic to which the whole family has looked forward all through the busy spring season. The picnic basket may take on all the gala atmosphere of the day, whether packed for a big neighborhood gathering or for a family picnic dinner at a nearby lake or town celebration.

A red, white, and blue color scheme is quite as possible at a picnic as at home. Paper napkins with colors of the day take place in the color idea. Sandwiches wrapped in oiled paper and tied with narrow red ribbon have the two-fold advantage of keeping fresh and being attractive. Pimiento, beets, and a dash of paprika, all add the red of our flag to the meat or salad dish. Blueberry muffins and cakes decorated with red candies carry the color of the lunch to dessert, and who would have a Fourth of July picnic without red (or "pink") lemonade!

A custom so old that it is almost a tradition, in the South especially, is the Fourth of July barbecue held when the crops are "laid by," and the choicest lamb and fattest shoat are barbecued over a pit of coals at the neighborhood picnic grounds. A miniature variation of this custom is the delightful and appetite-provoking lamb chops and steak broiled or barbecued over the bed of coals from a campfire, or the favorite fish fry, especially suited to smaller groups.

If a real picnic is not possible, why not pack the basket anyway and have the Fourth of July dinner out under a big shade tree in the yard?

—The Farmer's Wife Magazine, *July 1922*

❦ Fourth O' July Picnic Menu

Anna Coyle
July 1922

Picnic Sandwiches
The Farmer's Wife's *take on the classic BLT.*

12 slices bread, ¼-inch thick
butter to spread
1 small head lettuce
2 tomatoes
6–12 slices crisp bacon
salt and pepper

Spread bread with butter, stack slices with buttered sides together, and wrap in oiled paper or a napkin. Separate the lettuce leaves, wash well, place in a fruit jar, sprinkle with cold water, and screw on the lid of the jar. This method of carrying the lettuce will keep it fresh and crisp. When ready to spread lunch, the sandwiches are made up with a lettuce leaf, a thin slice of tomato, a slice or two of bacon, and a dash of salt and pepper between the slices of buttered bread. This sandwich adds just that cool crispness so welcome on a hot day.

Minced Ham Sandwiches

½ c. chopped ham
1 hard-boiled egg
3 tbsp. lemon juice
¼ tsp. prepared mustard
4 tbsp. melted butter
12 slices bread, buttered

Mix all together and use as a filling between the slices of bread. If more liquid is needed to moisten the mixture, cream may be added. Shredded lettuce is sometimes added to the mixture. Wrap each sandwich in wax paper.

Fourth of July Lemonade

3 lemons
1–3 c. sugar
1 c. purple grape juice
6 c. water

Squeeze the juice from the lemons, add the sugar, and let it dissolve, then add the grape juice. Pour into thermos bottle and finish filling bottle with cracked ice or cold water. The additional cold water to dilute will be added when ready to serve.

Patriotic Cakes

½ c. unsalted butter
½ c. sugar
4 eggs, well beaten
2 oz. bittersweet chocolate, melted
1 c. breadcrumbs
3 tbsp. flour

Cream the butter, then add sugar and well-beaten eggs. Stir in the chocolate, crumbs, and flour. Spread the mixture in a shallow, buttered pan and bake in a slow oven, at 325°F, until just golden. When done, cut with a biscuit cutter and ice each cake with white icing. For the Fourth of July picnic basket, decorate with little red candies forming the outline of an Independence Bell.

Barbecued Lamb Chops

2 tbsp. butter
¼ c. currant jelly
1 tbsp. vinegar
¼ tbsp. French mustard
cayenne and salt
12 lamb chops

Use a frying pan in which to melt the butter and jelly over the campfire.
Add vinegar, mustard, cayenne, and salt. Cut long green twigs and sharpen at
one end. Thrust the sharpened end through the chop, smear the sauce over
the chops, and hold over campfire to cook. The most satisfactory broiling
fire is one which has burned low, leaving a good bed of red coals. As the
chop cooks, apply the sauce two or three times with a dauber made by
tying a small piece of clean cheesecloth to a stick.

-OR-

Steak Gypsy Fashion

Have the campfire low, with a good bed of red coals. Sharpen green willow
sticks at each end. The large end is driven into the ground a short distance
from the fire and the steak is skewered to the small end. One small steak
for each person to be served is desirable. Two twigs are required for each
steak, and when in place, they extend over the fire and hold the meat in
position to broil. Turn the steak when well browned on one side. Serve
at once with plenty of butter, salt, and pepper to season. A delicate garlic
flavor is imparted by rubbing the dish on which the meat is placed with
the freshly cut face of a garlic clove. Potatoes baked in the embers are a
delightful accompaniment to this steak, and the same fire will cook both.

Cooking Out of Doors

Picnic suppers out-of-doors are a jolly way to end busy summer days. The companionship that comes from sharing supper duties about a campfire, and the stories or quiet talk which follow, become treasured memories for children and parents as well. It is not necessary that these pleasant experiences be limited to campers only; for the farm wood lot at dusk serves as well as a distant forest. Outdoor suppers may be quickly planned and may be as balanced and as easy to prepare as meals at home. In many family groups the older children take responsibility for cooking under the guidance of mother and father. Each child has his own duty, as carrying the food, gathering wood for the fire, cooking, and building the fire. One-dish meals have a rightfully deserved place of honor in the family outdoor supper plans. Such foods as tomatoes, rice, corn, eggs, cheese, and bacon offer many possibilities for delicious combinations.

—The Farmer's Wife Magazine

AN OPEN AIR FIREPLACE
September 1936

Must all meals be eaten in the house? Not if you ask the Paul Smith family, living on a large farm near Amenia, North Dakota. Especially not when it is so much fun to pick up the coffee pot and a few other necessities and hie out to an outdoor fireplace in the yard.

An impromptu picnic like the one shown in the picture can be planned on the spur of the moment, and it's fun. The Smiths not only find this enjoyable for their own family but have noticed that guests like it.

To save running back and forth to the house for the salt shaker, the bacon, or what not, Mrs. Smith loads everything into the hamper seen beside her. This fireplace is easily built and efficient. It consists merely of cement blocks (the upright ones serving as a chimney) and a piece of sheet iron for a cooking surface.

The Book Shelf

July 1929

No one need be lonesome in the summer time when he can have a good book to read. Everyday Adventures, *by Samuel Scoville, Jr., is a delightful book of woodland adventures and causes you to thrill at the discovery of the crimson vein sac of the pink lady-slipper or the swinging, pouch-like nest of the Baltimore oriole. An unusual nature book that will be welcomed by all nature lovers.*

OUTDOOR COOKERY
June 1935
Miriam J. Williams

"Let's do this again *soon*." So we all agreed, even though we were well seasoned with wood smoke, our shoes were dusty, our stockings burred, and our hands the grubbiest you ever saw. There's something about an outdoor picnic which is immensely satisfying, whether it's up a canyon, down by the creek, or over in the summer pasture or park where fires are allowed.

Planning ahead for interest and variety in the food is one way of making an outdoor meal a success. Wieners and buns are all right, but real outdoor enthusiasts have left that kind of picnic far, far behind. And they don't fry chicken and bake a cake before they leave home. Picnic-avoiders are usually those who figure that it means a lot of fuss, and yet the coffee is always muddy.

Of course picnic lovers go prepared. They aren't worrying over runs in silk stockings or a too-thin wrap. They don't lug along a lot of things they don't need. If good water isn't available at the camping site, they have brought some from home in jugs or jars. The skillet and pail used over the fire are well coated outside with soap or grease from a bacon rind so that they will clean easily. There are extra newspapers and plenty of paper napkins. Vegetables have been washed at home, and someone makes sure the kit includes matches and at least one sharp knife.

It's extremely handy to have a Camp Fire Girl or Boy or Girl Scout along, or at least one of their manuals to consult, because they know how to build and care for fires. And as for the meals which these enterprising girls and boys can prepare, they are different and delicious, well balanced and simple. Family meals eaten out-of-doors will be more successful if civilization lends its knives and forks, and cups which leave lips unscalded when used for hot chocolate or coffee. Sturdy paper plates are usually very acceptable and mean fewer sticky dishes for the kitchen sink. But let the young folks go "native" and see what can be done with nature's aids.

An easy way out for adults who don't want to bother with much cooking but like to eat around a campfire is to prepare a hot casserole at home, wrapping it in several layers of newspapers. At the camp site coffee is quickly made. With carrot and cucumber sticks or tomatoes for a salad, rolls, and a simple dessert, everyone is happy.

A favorite with young hikers are "kabobs" or "bobs." These are fashioned of cubes of meat or fish—lamb, beef, liver, oysters, whole shrimps—threaded on a pointed stick with alternate squares of sliced bacon and onion between. These are broiled over coals until done, with frequent turning. Cheese and bacon or banana and bacon are other "bob" possibilities. If you wish to add potato, they are most satisfactory if parboiled ten minutes, since they require longer cooking than meat.

These dishes will appeal to campers as well as picnickers.

❧ Kabobs
August 1929

Although half the fun in eating out of doors lies in cooking over the fire, one does not always wish to pack along even the useful frying pan. For these occasions, there are a number of good things which may be prepared without cooking utensils of any kind. One of the best is kabobs, favored of all campers. For each kabob is needed: a ¼-lb. beef steak, two or three slices onion, and one strip bacon. Plan for two kabobs for each person. Everyone will need a strong, pointed green stick. Then, alternate squares of beef and pieces of onion. Last of all, thread other end of bacon over stick. Roast over hot coals (never over blazing fire); when outside is browned, cook more slowly. Eat with graham rolls or bread.

Corn and Salmon Fritters

June 1935

1 14 or 14½-oz. can salmon
1 small can corn
¼ c. catsup
12 small crackers, crumbled fine

2 eggs, beaten slightly
½ tsp. salt
6 slices bacon, cut in half

Flake salmon and combine with all ingredients except bacon. Fry half the bacon, then remove; drop batter by spoonfuls in hot bacon fat and fry till golden brown on both sides. Repeat, using rest of bacon and rest of batter.

Angels on Horseback

August 1929

For this recipe of cheese with bacon (Angels on Horseback) we are grateful to the Girl Guides, English sisters of our own Girl Scouts. One-inch cubes of cheese are wrapped with a slice of bacon. This may be done so that the point of the green cooking stick holds the bacon firmly around the cheese during roasting. When the bacon is crisp, the "angel" is quite done and should be quickly popped into a roll. A lettuce leaf should be added to each roll. Plan for two "angels" per person.

Blushing Bunny

June 1935
From the Girl Scouts "Day Hikes"

1 tbsp. butter
1 tbsp. flour
1 can tomato soup
½ c. diced cheddar cheese
crackers

Melt butter, blend in flour, then add soup. When thoroughly heated, add cheese and stir till melted. Serve over crackers.

❧ Baked Potatoes or Corn
June 1933

Coat whole potato with thick layer of wet mud or clay. Toss into the fire and let bake about 45 minutes. Corn may be roasted on the ear by the same method as potatoes. The husk should be left on until the corn is cooked.

Clean freshly caught trout, allowing one or two fish for each serving. Wash, drain, and roll in flour, cornmeal, or cracker meal seasoned with salt and pepper. Fry in skillet over campfire with not too hot a flame, cooking gently for 10–15 minutes and turning once.

❧ Camp Fried Potatoes
June 1935

2 lbs. potatoes
1 or 2 onions
⅓ c. bacon or other fat
salt and pepper

Pare and slice potatoes into thin strips. Let soak in cold water till ready, then drain thoroughly. Slice onions. Put half the fat in hot skillet, add half potatoes and onions, and sprinkle with salt and pepper until beginning to brown and get clear. Push to one side, add remaining fat, potatoes, and onions and cook till all are done and nicely browned.

❦ Trout Fried in Butter

August 1938

Another picnic lunch eaten on the bank of Red Lake, Minnesota, might have taken a prize for little work and real enjoyment. Raw fried potatoes, fried fish, bread and butter, jelly sandwiches, pickles, gingerbread, milk, and coffee made up the menu. Those proficient in fire building and camp cookery prepared the fish, potatoes, and coffee, while others attended to laying the cloth and placing the food. Everyone enjoyed the eating and no one objected to the necessary dishwashing with the lake for a dishpan.

—The Farmer's Wife Magazine, June 1921

❦ Roasted Apples

June 1933

apples
brown sugar

Thrust pointed end of green stick into core of apple and roast slowly before brisk fire, turning occasionally. Eat with brown sugar.

❦ An Outdoor Dessert

August 1929

Also known as . . . s'mores.

An out-of-doors dessert which is easily made consists of sandwiches made of graham crackers, ⅓ bar of sweet chocolate, and two marshmallows. Put chocolate on graham cracker, toast marshmallows, place above chocolate, and add second cracker.

SUNRISE BREAKFAST IN THE WOODS
UP BEFORE DAWN AND OUT WITH THE
BIRDS—WILL YOU DO IT?
Jean Hathaway

For real fun and complete enjoyment of a hearty breakfast, nothing could possibly surpass a sunrise breakfast in the woods or beside a lake or stream. Preparations are all made the day before, baskets are packed and, at the early hour fixed upon, a gay group of girls gathers at the appointed meeting place and begins to hike to the spot where breakfast is to be cooked over a campfire. Every girl from the age of twelve to—well, let's not set a limit—has been invited, and if the boys promise to help with the bonfire, they may come, too.

The hike is to the slope at the edge of a wonderful stretch of timber just two miles away. There is a promise of sizzly bacon, fried potatoes, Mother's best rolls, and all the good, rich cocoa you can drink. The bacon, to be at its best, must be sliced almost as thin as paper. The potatoes are brought boiled and sliced to make it easy to reheat them in the frying pan. Everyone is expected to carry a pint of milk for cocoa, unless some kind person volunteers to deliver enough for all at the scene of action.

Before breakfast, setting up exercises: everyone gathers firewood and helps with the breakfast. Then everyone eats. After breakfast, games and the hike home before the August sun reaches its height.

Drinks

Beverages that Refresh

By Mabel K. Ray
July 1932

On a sweltering summer day, who wouldn't like a crispy something to crunch and a beverage with a clink of ice in it? Nothing, absolutely nothing, is more refreshing—or at least that is the way many feel about it.

And when you come to all kinds of drinks, there is such a vast array that a different one could be served almost every day in the year. Fruit drinks, milk drinks, malt-cocoa fruit drinks, coffee drinks, and tea drinks are just a few of the appetizing ones.

To get the "crunch," cheese sticks, fattigmands, graham crackers, salted crackers, and other wafers meet the requirements. The recipes? Here they are!

❦ Rhubarb Punch

July 1932
Contributed by S.D.A.C.

3 c. rhubarb
3 c. water
1½ c. sugar
1 c. orange juice
3 tbsp. lemon juice
2 c. ice water

Cook rhubarb, cut in small pieces without peeling, in 3 c. water until very soft. Rub through a fine strainer, add sugar, and stir until it dissolves. Chill. Add fruit juice and ice water and pour into glasses. This makes six glasses.

Independence Day Punch
July 1936
Contributed by Mrs. C.B., Missouri

2 qts. sugar
1 qt. water
2 qts. infusion of orange pekoe tea
1 qt. lemon juice (15-18 lemons)
1 qt. orange juice (8-12 oranges)
1 qt. grape juice

1 large can crushed pineapple
2 gal. ice water
1 c. strawberry or banana slices
1 c. thin orange slices
ice

Boil sugar with water to make a syrup and cool. To make tea infusion, pour 2 qts. boiling water over ½ c. orange pekoe tea. Let stand 5 minutes and strain from leaves. Add fruit juices, fruit, water, and syrup, and pour over blocks of ice. Makes 4 gallons punch and serves 60 large glasses, 120 small ones.

Please! When you light your firecrackers, will you throw them away quickly? If one does not go off after it is lit, will you leave it lying where it is for a long time? Will you be very careful not to throw a firecracker at any person? July 4th is a good time for "Safety First."

—The Farmer's Wife Magazine

❧ Ginger Milk Punch

July 1932

To be made with very fresh farm eggs only!

2 eggs, separated	⅛ tsp. salt
2 tbsp. sugar	2 c. milk
1 tbsp. fresh grated ginger	nutmeg for dusting

Beat the yolks, then add the sugar, ginger, and salt. Mix well, then add milk. Pour over stiffly beaten egg whites, dust with nutmeg, and serve well iced.

❧ Cold Cocoa Milk

July 1932

3 tbsp. cocoa syrup
¾ c. cold milk

Add cocoa syrup to milk and beat briskly with an egg beater (or mix in the blender).

Tomatoes, it is said, will quench thirst five times more effectually than water, so doubtless some experimenter is now at work on cold tomato drinks.

—The Farmer's Wife Magazine

❧ Switchel

August 1923

This is a favorite summer drink for the eastern haymaker and harvester. Put 1 tsp. sugar, ¹⁄₁₆ tsp. powdered ginger, and 2 tsp. boiled cider in a glass and fill with water. Vinegar and molasses may be substituted for boiled cider, half and half.

❦ Cereal Drinks
August 1923

A handful of raw oatmeal or rolled oats in a quart of water "goes pretty good," the men say. Sometimes a little lemon juice and sugar may be added, but no real thirst quencher should be really sweet. And it is safer not to be ice cold.

❦ Raspberry Shrub
August 1923

1 qt. vinegar
3 qts. raspberries (red are best), crushed
sugar

Pour the vinegar over the crushed raspberries and let stand overnight. Strain through a jelly bag. To each pt. measure juice add an equal amount of sugar. Boil 20 minutes. Use ¼ c. of shrub to each glass and fill with water.

❦ Shrub Punch
August 1923

1 c. sugar
1 c. water
2 c. Raspberry Shrub (see above)
½ c. lemon juice
1 c. tea infusion (steep 1 bag in 1 c. boiling water)
1 c. canned pineapple syrup
1 pt. ginger ale

Boil the sugar and water together for 5 minutes. Add other ingredients. Just before serving add the ginger ale to give zest and sparkle. To be at its best, punch must be ice cold. All sorts of punches may be made from one foundation.

❦ Foundation Punch

August 1923

4 oranges

2 lemons

1 c. sugar

½ c. water

Squeeze the juice from the oranges and lemons. Boil the sugar and water to the thread stage. Add fruit juice and water to make 2 qts. 1 c. chopped mint leaves may be steeped in boiling water, strained, and substituted for part of the water.

Variety is gained by adding other fruit juices, sweetening if necessary with more of the syrup.

Berry Punch: Equal parts foundation punch and berry syrup.

Cherry or Currant Punch: Three parts foundation to one part cherry or currant juice.

Ginger Punch: Boil ½ lb. cut ginger in the foundation punch.

Grape Punch: Equal parts foundation punch and grape juice.

❦ Root Beer Fruit Ade

July 1932

Root beer extract is available at specialty and gourmet shops, as well as from a number of online purveyors.

2 tsp. root beer extract

4 tbsp. or more sugar to
  sweeten to taste

Juice of 1 lemon, 1 orange,
  or ¼ c. pineapple

2 qts. ice cold water

Mix extract thoroughly with the sugar; then, and not until then, add the fruit juice and the water. Stir well and serve. To make a larger quantity increase proportions proportionately. A bottled root beer drink is easily made and refreshing. Root beer extracts are made of various roots and herbs.

❦ Iced Coffee
July 1932

Make coffee a little stronger than usual to allow for dilution by ice (1½ tbsp. coffee to a cup). Pour hot coffee over ice in individual glasses. Use powdered sugar for sweetening and cream as desired. It may be topped off with whipped cream. Left-over coffee cannot be expected to make good iced coffee.

❦ Coffee Milk Shake
July 1932

Coffee syrup is available at specialty and gourmet shops, as well as from a number of online purveyors. Or you can make your own; recipe follows.

3 tbsp. Coffee Syrup (see below)
¾ c. whole milk
2 drops vanilla extract
ice

Shake or stir vigorously and serve. To make eggnog, add one egg to the ingredients before serving.

Coffee Syrup:
2 c. extra-strong coffee
3½ lbs. sugar

Boil two to three minutes. Store in refrigerator till ready to use.

University of Vermont Cold Milk Drinks
August 1923

Many people who object to milk as a beverage find it delicious if flavorings are added. Charged water or Vichy [water] adds greatly to the flavor of the following but may be omitted. The flavorings may be prepared by making a thick syrup and adding any fruit juice, chocolate, cocoa, vanilla, and so forth. This syrup should be highly flavored in order to have a small quantity sufficient for a glass of milk. A mild-flavored fruit juice may be improved by the addition of a little lemon, rhubarb, or other very acid juice.

Chocolate Syrup

2 c. sugar
1 c. water
2 oz. bittersweet chocolate
½ tsp. vanilla

Boil sugar in the water until it is dissolved. Melt the chocolate and add syrup slowly, stirring constantly. Bring to the boiling point, then cool and add vanilla. Store in glass jar for use. ¼ lb. cocoa may be substituted for the chocolate.

Fruit Syrup

Omit extract and substitute juice for three-quarters of the water called for. This makes a better syrup.

Milk Blossom

2 tbsp. syrup
½ glass milk
charged water

Place syrup in glass and fill with charged water or use milk alone. Ice cream or whipped cream may be used as a float.

Mint Julep

1 egg
2 tbsp. mint syrup
½ glass milk
charged water (as above)

To the well-beaten egg add syrup, milk, and water. Beat thoroughly.

Buttermilk Lemonade

Combine 1 qt. buttermilk with the juice of three lemons (or part orange juice) and sweeten to taste.

❦ Unfermented Grape Juice
August 1911

Add 1 qt. water to 3 qts. grapes, stemmed and washed, boil until soft, and strain. Bring to a boil again, then cool. Store in refrigerator till ready to use, and serve diluted with water or over cracked ice, sweetened to taste.

COOLING DRINKS FOR SUMMER
August 1912
Elma Iona Locke

There are many delicious cooling beverages that may be made with little trouble at home, and especially the various kinds made from fruit should be freely used during the hot weather. But iced drinks should seldom be indulged in, especially at meal time or soon after, as they chill the stomach and check digestion. The pleasant acidity of fruit juices, together with pure cold water, are sufficiently cooling for health.

❦ Soda Water
August 1912

1 oz. tartaric acid	1 egg white
1 lb. sugar	2 tbsp. lemon, vanilla, or
1 pt. boiling water	pineapple extract

Mix all together in an earthen bowl, stir briskly, and pour into bottles, storing in refrigerator until ready to use. Shake well before using. Into a glassful of water stir 2 tbsp. of the mixture and ¼ tsp. baking soda. This makes a foamy drink.

❦ A Temperance Mint Julep
August 1912

Thoroughly crush one bunch of mint, then soak it for ½ hour in the strained juice of two lemons, adding the grated rind of one and being careful not to get in any of the white skin. Boil 1 pt. water with 1 lb. sugar till the syrup spins a thread. Take it from the fire and stir in the lemon and mint, the juice of an orange, and pineapple juice in an equal amount to the orange. Strain and cool.

❦ Lemonade
August 1912

Wash the lemons well before using, scrubbing them lightly with a small brush; rinse and dry. Roll them until soft and grate off the yellow rind, being careful not to get any of the bitter white skin. Cut the lemons in two and squeeze out the juice, adding 2 oz. sugar and 1 qt. water to three lemons. Let stand for half an hour and add a freshly cut slice of lemon to each glass. The water may be poured boiling hot over the lemon and sugar then cooled, if wished.

Fourth of July

ON THE Fourth of July, if the sun
   shines,
The big celebration can be.
In the day there'll be picnics and
   speeches.
At night there'll be fireworks to see.

If it rains on the Fourth of July day
It will spoil all the picnics and then
The Fourth of July celebration
Can't be till July comes again.

If the rain cared to come the day after
It then wouldn't bother a bit.
I could rest from the big celebration
And spend the day thinking of it.

❦ Whey Lemonade

July 1932

Made your own cheese lately? Then you likely have some whey on hand—the watery liquid leftover after cheese curds are formed. It's an excellent source of protein and, for the farmer's wife, a nutritive addition to this summer beverage.

1 qt. whey
6 tbsp. sugar
juice of 2 lemons
slices of lemon or a little grated rind
nutmeg or cinnamon

Mix all together, chill, and serve.

❦ Milk Lemonade

August 1911

Dissolve 3 c. sugar in 1 qt. boiling water, then add 1 c. strained lemon juice and set away to cool. When cold, add 1½ pts. fresh milk. Shake well and place on ice. Serve ice cold, pouring it several times from one vessel to another.

☙ Orangeade
August 1912

Grate the yellow rind from two oranges and squeeze out the juice, adding 2 oz. sugar, the juice of one lemon, and 1 pt. water.

☙ Pineapple Lemonade
August 1912

Peel, eye, and grate one large, ripe pineapple. Add the strained juice of four lemons and a syrup made by boiling 1 lb. sugar and 1 pt. water together for 3–4 minutes. When cold, add 1 qt water and strain.

☙ Currantade
August 1912

Take 1 pt. ripe red currants and ½ pt. red raspberries and crush them with sugar to sweeten. Let stand for half an hour, then add 2 qts. cold water and strain.

☙ Raspberryade
July–August 1921

1 c. raspberry juice
2 tsp. lemon juice
1 c. water
1 tsp. sugar
3 bruised mint leaves

Stir until sugar is dissolved and place on ice to cool.

❧ Grapeade
August 1912

Press the juice from 2 lbs. Catawba grapes, strain, and add to the juice 3 tbsp. sugar and 1 glass cold water, stirring until the sugar is dissolved.

❧ Fruit Punch
July 1917

1 pt. freshly made black tea
6 lemons
12 oranges
1 c. prune juice
2 c. pineapple juice
2 c. strawberry juice
1 c. sugar syrup
2 qt. water

Extract the juice from the lemons and oranges, add the other fruit juices, and strain. Add the sugar syrup and water. Refrigerate till ready to use, then add to tea. Dilute with plain or carbonated water to suit the taste.

❦ Iced Tea
August 1919

1 qt. boiling water	4 slices lemon
4 level tsp. tea	ice

Pour boiling water over tea, cover closely, and let stand to steep about 3 minutes. Then pour off the tea from the leaves and let stand till cold. For serving, add cracked ice and a slice of lemon to each glass and let each person sweeten the tea to taste; tall glasses are best for iced tea in order to hold the ice.

❦ Fruited Tea
August 1928

1 qt. fresh drawn boiling water	6 whole cloves
2 level tsp. black tea	

Pour water over tea and cloves and allow to stand 3 minutes. Pour off water and chill thoroughly. For each glass add:

1 slice lemon	1 slice orange
1 maraschino cherry, cut in	speck preserved or
small portions	crystallized ginger

❦ Minted Tea
August 1928

1½ qts. boiling water
1 level tbsp. orange pekoe tea
4–5 mint leaves

Pour water over tea and mint leaves and allow to stand 3 minutes. Pour off liquid and chill, and serve with a fresh mint leaf and a slice of orange in each glass.

🌾 Spiced Syrup for Punch or Iced Tea

July 1935

2 c. sugar
1 c. water
1 tsp. whole cloves
3-inch stick cinnamon

Bring sugar and water to boil and boil 1 minute. Add spice, cover, and let stand till cool. Strain out spice before using. Use one-third to half as much spiced syrup as freshly made tea, and use with lemon juice or other tart fruit juices for punch. Or add just enough syrup to sweeten iced tea.

🌾 Picnic Coffee

July 1919

Allow 1 tbsp. rounded measure of coffee for each guest to be served. Measure coffee into a bowl. Add the white of one egg for every seven persons to be served. Stir all together thoroughly until the coffee is evenly wet. Put in clean glass jars, cover tightly, and it is ready to carry to the picnic. To make the coffee, add to this mixture, in the pot, 1 large coffee cup of freshly drawn clean water for each guest. Stir grounds and water till well mixed and put on to boil. Let boil hard for 3–5 minutes and *do not let it boil over.* Remove from the fire and let stand a few minutes to settle.

🌾 Maple Cream

August 1919

4 tbsp. maple syrup
2 tbsp. cream
ginger ale

Put the maple syrup and cream into a glass. Pour in the ice cold ginger ale to nearly fill the glass. Beat hard with a spoon and serve.

Index

Angel Food Cake, 106
Angels on Horseback, 204
Apple and Celery Salad, 144
Apple Batter Pudding, 95
Apple Brown Betty, 148
Apple Cake, 149
Apple Cobbler, 147
Apple Fritters, 19
Apple Frost, 146
Apple Injun, 148
Apple Pie, 101
Apple Salad, 187
Apple Snow, 146
Applesauce, 150
Applesauce Cheese Tarts, 150
Baked Acorn Squash, 120
Baked Bananas, 112
Baked Cabbage, 153
Baked Eggs and Greens, 35
Baked Hominy and Cheese, 75
Baked Onions, 88
Baked Potatoes or Corn, 205
Baked Rice, 83
Baked Southampton Ham, 65
Baked Stuffed Green
  Peppers, 118
Baked Summer Squash and
  Corn, 121
Baking Powder Biscuits, 52
Banana Bread, 26
Banana Cake, 111
Banana Cream Pie, 102
Banana Pudding, 96
Barbecued Lamb Chops, 199
Basic Honey Cake, 112
Beef Cakes with Brown
  Gravy, 56
Beef Stew, 61
Beets and Greens with Sour
  Sauce, 152
Beets and Onion Supreme, 152
Blackberry Gingerbread
  Upside-Down Cake, 126
Blackberry Pudding, 127
Blackberry Roly-poly, 126
Blushing Bunny, 204
Boiled Corn, 132
Boston Baked Beans, 84
Bread Dumplings, 69
Bread Omelet, 35
Bread Pudding, 95
Bread Sticks, 166
Breakfast Cocoa, 18
Broiled Hamburgers, 57
Brood Khutjes, 69
Brunswick Stew, 52
Butterhorn Rolls, 45
Buttermilk Lemonade, 215
Buttermilk Pie, 100

Cabbage Salad, 183, 192
Camp Fried Potatoes, 205
Cantaloupe as Dessert, 139
Cauliflower au Gratin, 144
Cereal Drinks, 211
Cheese and Pimiento
  Sandwiches, 173
Cheese Straws, 166
Cherry Batter Pudding, 94
Cherry Cream Pie, 103
Chicken Casserole with
  Biscuits, 55
Chicken Goulash, 54
Chicken Pie, 51
Chicken Salad, 186
Chicken Sandwich, 170
Chicken Shortcake, 53
Chicken with Dumplings, 51
Chile Sauce, 37
Chili, 59
Chocolate Sauce for Ice
  Cream, 115
Chocolate Syrup, 214
Chopped Ham Filling, 172
Cinnamon Rolls, 28
Cocoanut Cream Pie, 103
Coffee Cake, 28
Coffee Milk Shake, 213
Coffee Syrup, 213
Cold Cocoa Milk, 210
Cold Slaw, 184
Compote of Apples, 147
Cooked Raisin Filling, 174
Corn and Pepper Sauté, 85
Corn and Salmon Fritters, 204
Corn Bread, 75
Corn Fritters, 19
Corn Pudding, 96
Corn Salad, 134
Corn Scramble, 33
Corn Soufflé, 133
Cornmeal Spoon Bread, 74
Cottage Cheese Fillings, 179
Cottage Cheese Pie, 102
Country Kitchen Salad, 185
Cracked Wheat Bread, 43
Cranberry and Raisin Pie, 154
Cream Gravy for Fried
  Chicken, 50
Cream of Corn Soup, 132
Cream of Tomato Soup, 137
Creamed Eggs and Bacon on
  Toast, 34
Creamed Onion Tops, 88
Crème de Menthe Pears, 156
Creole Green Corn, 85
Crisp Crumb Torte, 107
Cuban Chicken, 54
Cucumber Sandwiches, 172

Currantade, 219
Curried Brisket, 61
Date and Nut Bread with
  Cream Cheese Filling, 177
Date Bars, 168
Delicious Apple
  Dumplings, 145
Denver Sandwiches, 177
Devil's Food Cake, 110
Deviled Eggs, 164
Different Bacon, 18
Dutch Lettuce Slaw, 119
Easy Chocolate Cookies, 167
Easy Fattigmands, 164
Egg Sandwiches, 171, 191
Eggs à la King, 34
Escalloped Eggplant with
  Tomatoes and Onions, 153
Escalloped Ham and
  Potatoes, 67
Escalloped Potatoes in Tomato
  Sauce, 78
Foundation Punch, 212
Foundation Recipe for
  Muffins, 24
Fourth of July Lemonade, 198
Frankfurter Crown, 71
French Fried Onions, 88
French Fruit Toast, 32
French Salad Dressing, 181
French Toast, 31
French Vanilla Ice Cream, 114
Fried Apples, 147
Fried Corn, 133
Fried Cucumbers, 134
Fried Green Tomatoes, 136
Fried Tomatoes, 136
Frosted Berries, 127
Fruit and Nut Sandwiches, 173
Fruit Cobbler, 99
Fruit Pie, 104
Fruit Punch, 220
Fruit Salad, 187
Fruit Sandwiches, 191
Fruit Syrup, 214
Fruited Tea, 221
German Kuchen, 28
German Potato Salad, 188
Ginger Milk Punch, 210
Ginger Snaps, 167
Glaceéd Sweet Potatoes, 157
Gooseberry Fool, 129
Gooseberry Trifle, 129
Graham Muffins, 25
Grapeade, 220
Grapefruit Salad, 188
Gravy, 70
Ham and Sour Cream
  Casserole, 66

Ham Omelet, 36
Ham Sandwiches, 191
Ham Succotash in
    Casserole, 66
Hard Sauce, 127
Harvest Layer Cake, 155
Honey Apricot Straws, 165
Honey Bran Flake Muffins, 25
Huckleberry Pudding, 151
Huevos Rancheros, 37
Iced Coffee, 213
Iced Tea, 221
Independence Day Punch, 209
Italian Squash, 120
Kabobs, 203
Knedliky, 76
Knepp, 68
Lamb Stew, 70
Lemon "Cake" Pie, 104
Lemonade, 217
Lettuce and Onion
    Sandwiches, 172
Lettuce Sandwich, 173
Lima Beans in Casserole, 87
Loose Meat Sandwiches, 60
Macaroni with Minced
    Ham, 67
Maple Cream, 222
Maple Parfait, 115
Marguerites, 165
Mayonnaise Dressing, 181
Meat Loaf, 60
Meringue, 140
Milk Blossom, 215
Milk Lemonade, 218
Minced Ham Sandwiches, 197
Mint Julep, 215
Minted Tea, 221
Miss Linda's Hoecakes, 74
Norwegian Cloob, 83
Oatmeal with Bran, 18
Old-Fashioned Strawberry
    Shortcake, 125
Olive Sandwiches, 175
One-Pot Meal, 192
Onion Juice, 57
Orange Biscuits, 29
Orangeade, 219
Original Salmon and Potato
    Loaf with Mushroom
    Sauce, 73
Outdoor Dessert, 206
Oven Fried Potatoes, 77
Patriotic Cakes, 198
Pea and Carrot Casserole, 90
Pea Soufflé, 90
Peach Custard Pie, 140
Peach Dumplings, 139
Peach Pudding, 97
Peach Soufflé, 140
Peanut Brittle Ice Cream, 114
Peanut Butter Bread, 168
Peanut Butter Fillings, 178
Peanut Butter Toast, 32
Peas, 89

Pennsylvania Rice Pudding, 98
Pepper Pot, 69
Peppermint Ice Cream, 114
Picnic Coffee, 222
Picnic Pie, 193
Picnic Sandwiches, 197
Pies for a Week, 101
Pimiento Relish, 143
Pineapple Lemonade, 219
Pineapple Upside-Down
    Cake, 108
Pineapples and Strawberries
    with Mint, 125
Plain Pastry, 100
Plum Cream Pie, 141
Plum Salad, 141
Popovers, 46
Pork Chop Casserole, 62
Pork-and-Bean Pie with Sweet
    Potato Topping, 62
Pot Roast and Noodles, 59
Potato Cakes, 77
Potato Dumplings, 83
Potato Knedliky, 76
Potato Muffins, 25
Potato Pancakes, 79
Pumpkin Butter, 158
Pumpkin Pie Filling, 158
Quick Graham Bread, 42
Radish Sandwich, 172
Raised Dumplings, 68
Raspberry Cream, 128
Raspberry Pudding Sauce, 128
Raspberry Shrub, 211
Raspberryade, 219
Raw Carrot Salad, 143
Rhode Island Johnny Cakes, 30
Rhubarb Crisp, 99
Rhubarb Punch, 208
Rice Cakes, 30
Roast Beef Supreme, 56
Roast Stuffed Spareribs, 64
Roast Turkey, 159
Roasted Apples, 206
Root Beer Fruit Ade, 212
Sage Stuffing, 63
Sallie's Rye Dough Dabs, 20
Salmon Loaf, 195
Salmon Sandwiches, 173
Sandwich Filling, 172–174
Sausage Pudding, 69
Scalloped Potatoes, 78
Scalloped Sweet Potato and
    Apple, 157
Schnitz un Knepp, 68
Seven-Minute Icing, 110
Shredded Carrot Salad, 186
Shrub Punch, 211
Slappers, 31
Soda Water, 216
Sour Cream Cake with
    Variations, 109
Sour Cream Chocolate Ice
    Cream, 114
Sour Cream Crullers, 20

Sour Cream Dressing, 182
Sour Milk Biscuits, 21
Sour Milk Gingerbread, 107
Sour Milk Griddle Cakes, 29
Southern Fried Chicken, 50
Spanish Lima Beans, 87
Spiced Syrup for Punch or Iced
    Tea, 222
Steak Gypsy Fashion, 199
Steamed Brown Bread, 43
Steamed Chocolate Pudding
    with Sterling Sauce, 93
Steamed Cocoa Pudding, 97
Sterling Sauce, 93
Stewed Cabbage, 153
Strawberry Float, 124
Strawberry Ice Cream, 115
Strawberry Pudding, 123
Strawberry Trifle, 124
String Beans, 91
String Beans with Bacon, 91
Stuffed and Baked Pimientos,
    142
Stuffed Pork Tenderloin, 63
Stuffed Summer Squash, 121
Stuffed Sweet Potatoes, 157
Stuffed Tomatoes with
    Cheese, 136
Sweet Chocolate
    Sandwiches, 178
Sweet Potato Puff, 156
Sweet Rolls, 44
Switchel, 210
Tapioca Cream, 98
Temperance Mint Julep, 216
Texas Hash, 55
Thousand Island Dressing, 182
Toasted Cheese with Bacon, 33
Tomato Salad, 138
Tomato Sandwich, 170
Tomatoes in Batter, 137
Tomatoes on Toast, 138
Trout Fried in Butter, 206
Turkey Stuffing, 159
Turnips Delicious, 119
Two Good German Coffee
    Cakes, 27
Two-Tone Meatloaf, 194
Unfermented Grape Juice, 215
University of Vermont Cold
    Milk Drinks, 214
Vegetable Salad, 184, 192
Vegetable Sandwich
    Filling, 171
Waffles par Excellence, 31
Waldorf Filling, 173
Watercress, 122
Whey Lemonade, 218
Whipped Cream Filling, 173
White Sauce, 89
Whole Wheat Bread, 43
Zucchini, 120